The Process of Writing

Mary Riordan–Karlsson, Ed. D

Teacher Created Materials, Inc.

Cover Design by Darlene Spivak

Copyright © 1999 Teacher Created Materials, Inc. All rights reserved.

No part of this publication may be reproduced in whole or in part, or stored in any retrieval system, or transmitted in any form or by any means, electronic, mechanical, photocopying, recording, or otherwise, without written permission from the publisher, Teacher Created Materials, Inc., 6421 Industry Way, Westminster, CA 92683.

www.teachercreated.com

Reprinted, 1999
Made in U.S.A.

ISBN 1-57690-473-3

Order Number TCM 2473

Table of Contents

Introduction

Professional's Guide: The Process of Writing discusses the early phases of reading and writing before children enter into formal school settings and the emergence of their literacy skills in the classroom. Chapters highlight such topics as emergent literacy, reading and writing connections, becoming young authors, literacy activities at home, writing in the classroom, reading and writing activities for older children, and assessment principles. Throughout the chapters, examples across the curriculum are provided to support the ideas and perspectives of the constructivist theory that undergirds this book. Sample literacy activities are also included to help you begin to think about the amazing literacy journey your students embark on each day in your classroom.

I emphasize the process of writing, but that, by its nature, includes the reading that takes place during writing. I will discuss emergent literate behaviors in the home environment and in the classroom and ways to integrate reading and writing across the curriculum. Assessment principles are discussed as a way for you to envision alternative ways of evaluating your students' growth and progress as readers and writers.

As you read this book, I hope you will begin to understand more clearly the complexities inherent in the reading and writing processes. *The Process of Writing* offers you the opportunity to reflect on the teaching and learning processes and strategies for enhancing the educational experience for all of your students.

I want to thank the young authors, Meghan, Patrick, and Mary Kate for their contributions to this book to improve our understanding of the writing process.

Emergent Literacy

Understanding Emergent Literacy

Think about the importance of reading and writing in your life and reflect on the process that you went through to become a reader and a writer. Did you have a favorite book your mother or father read to you? Was there a favorite part of a story you acted out with your siblings or friends? What do you remember about your earliest writing experiences? Was it writing a birthday card to your brother or sister or a Mother's Day card for your mother? Was it a letter to Santa? As you reflect on your early literacy experiences, think about your own literacy journey and the miracle of reading and writing we often take for granted. These reflections are very important as you witness children becoming literate in your classroom every day. Teachers need to better understand the lifelong literacy journey their students embark upon and appreciate each step of their journey.

In the past two decades, new ways of conceptualizing the reading and writing development of young children have been the focus of much research, resulting in new standards. A new term, "emergent literacy," arose from this new perspective, which evolved in part from Marie Clay's (1966, 1967) influential research on young children learning about reading, writing, and print prior to formal schooling. Emergent literacy focuses on the earliest phases of literacy, the time period between birth and the time when children read and write conventionally. We now know that becoming literate is a continuous, lifelong process which begins in infancy with exposure to oral and written language through songs, books, alphabet blocks, and stories. The learning process begins in the home and branches out to other

> As you reflect on your early literacy experiences, think about your own literacy journey and the miracle of reading and writing we often take for granted.

environments, most importantly the school environment where children are formally taught how to communicate and use language in a multitude of ways. With a growing number of children entering a school-like setting, for example, preschool and Head Start, it is critical that teachers and caregivers who work with young children are aware of the research and practices that focus on emergent literacy.

Emergent literacy can be broadly defined as "the reading and writing behaviors that precede and develop into conventional literacy" (Sulzby, 1989, p. 83). The early years, from birth to around five years old, are critical in a child's literacy development. Emergent literate behaviors are demonstrated in many ways, such as pretending to read a favorite book, drawing a picture, writing a story, and writing one's own name. Often these behaviors are revealed during play with other children. Throughout this book the individual literacy behaviors of children as well as the literacy behaviors of children engaged in activities with others will be illustrated. To truly understand emergent literacy, we must first look at ways that literacy is acquired. Then discuss theories that view the teaching and learning processes through a social constructivist lens and consider the importance of the social world in the literacy development of a child.

> Emergent literacy can be broadly defined as "the reading and writing behaviors that precede and develop into conventional literacy" (Sulzby, 1989, p. 83).

An Emerging Goal

Emergent literacy has become a national concern and the improvement of reading and writing behaviors of young children has become a goal of teachers and caretakers in early childhood classrooms. The National Education Goals Report (1995) reads: Goal 1: Ready to Learn "By the year 2000, all children in America will start school ready to learn." The first objective states, "All children will have access to high-quality and developmentally appropriate preschool programs that help prepare children for school." This objective directly relates to the emergence of "emergent literacy" as a major area of focus for educators. The National Education Goals Report (1995) also states that "The proportion of preschoolers who are regularly read to and told stories has increased." This is a positive finding. As children are exposed to books and stories, their awareness of print increases, and they learn that written and oral language is a communication tool.

The Acquisition of Literacy

Literacy is a complex, multifaceted phenomenon which has perplexed parents, educators, and researchers for decades since there are many definitions and characteristics of literacy. It is known that literacy develops through every interaction and activity a child engages in. Children are active participants in their own development (Rogoff, 1990). The individual child, social partners, and the cultural milieu are inseparable contributors to the ongoing activities in which child development takes place. To become a member of a literate society, a child needs to participate in activities that are valued by the society. Therefore, both the social world a child lives in and the interactions and dialogues that he or she engages in greatly influence the reading and writing processes.

The acquisition of literacy occurs both in the home environment and in the school environment. The active role of the child in the process of learning to read and write is one perspective situated in an emergent literacy approach to literacy development. In understanding young children's literacy development, a look at the literacy activities the child engages in at home and at school sheds light on the role of the literacy acquisition process. Additionally, the context in which the activity takes place can impact early literacy development in multiple ways, particularly in children's perceptions of literacy, the nature of literacy events in diverse communities, and the discourse practices in home and in school.

A Social Constructivist Perspective of Learning

When learning is viewed through a social constructivist lens, we see how children learn and the processes by which they do so. It is extremely important to consider the context of the activity and the participants in the activity. We need to also examine what is learned through the social interaction and dialogues and how it helps the child learn to read, write, speak, and listen.

It is extremely important to consider the context of the activity and the participants in the activity.

From infancy on, we as human beings are remarkably social (Bruner, 1986) and through the process of socializing, learning occurs. Indeed, young children's literacy development is embedded in their social world and the social worlds of others. After all, literacy is a social accomplishment (Bloome, 1986; Dyson, 1990; Santa Barbara Discourse Group, Green et al.,1992), not an individual one. Children learn literacy skills through interactions with others, negotiating meaning, and reconceptualizing their ideas. Children are actively involved in their own development; they construct knowledge and negotiate meanings in a social context, and then their interpretations of the world are later internalized. This internalization process is only part of the learning process which is embedded within the social context. Another part of the learning process is the dialogue that surrounds the literacy activity. When a child writes a story, naturally he or she wants to read it to a friend or a parent. Likewise, when a child learns to read, he or she wants to read aloud or retell the story in his or her own words. Through social activities which include language use, reading texts and writing texts, learners construct new knowledge that builds on existing prior knowledge. With the assistance of others, children form new ideas that extend their pre-existing ideas.

Literacy is believed to be both an individual intellectual achievement and a form of cultural knowledge that enables people to participate in a range of groups and activities that in some way involve writing and reading (McLane & McNamee, 1990). Anne Dyson (1993), a leading researcher in children's writing, supports this viewpoint in defining literacy as a dialectic relationship involving children's use of print to represent their ideas and to interact with other people. To truly understand the development of literacy, we must look at the environments in which literacy is developed, the participants in the literacy activities, and the tools which are used.

The Importance of the Social World

> **Children are continuously seeking to figure out their places in the social world, in the classroom, at home, or among peers.**

Children are continuously seeking to figure out their places in the social world, in the classroom, at home, or among peers. They want to participate in the social world around them, which can be accomplished through talking or writing. Children can develop literacy skills through different interactions with peers and adults. There are numerous intellectual gains that are made through these interactions with various participants. When students from different backgrounds and different age groups work together, they each bring to the activity another set of tools which can be used to construct and negotiate meaning. All members of the group contribute to the construction of meaning and reconceptualize their own ideas which are then turned into written stories, poems, or plays.

The social worlds of children learning to read and write include the official community of the school, the enacted curriculum, and the interactions with the teacher and/or another adult in the classroom (Dyson, 1993). The other social world, then, is the unofficial peer world, which includes interactions and conversations with peers in the classroom. Throughout a child's educational career, he or she moves among these two worlds, thus learning how to negotiate and construct meaning from experiences within both the official world of the classroom and the unofficial world of peers.

Moreover, the context of the activity is equally as important as the activity itself. Children try to "make sense" and construct meaning through negotiations with others in various contexts, which helps them to re-think and re-work their ideas to formulate new knowledge.

Learning to use language effectively and learning to read and write begin at an early age and involve young children and the significant people in their lives, including parents, grandparents, aunts, uncles, teachers, and friends. The social world a child lives in provides a context in which meaning is constructed and negotiated with people who are important, such as family members, caretakers, and teachers, who model literacy activities in a context which is comfortable and inviting. Then, a child will be curious about participating in the social world and become an active member of the literate community.

Literacy is a cultural tool for taking action in the world, and that action is usually derived from an interaction between children and adults.

While it is commonly believed that literacy is developed independently, the social constructivist perspective, grounded in the work of Vygotsky (1978), a Russian theorist, and Vygotskian inspired scholars (e.g., Rogoff, 1990; Wertsch, 1985, 1991), provides an alternate view of literacy development. No longer is the focus on the individual; instead, the perspective has widened to view the individual participating with others in various literacy activities. Through this perspective, development is not a linear transformation of mental structures but situated changes in sociocognitive actions, in children's ways of participation in culturally valued activities. That is, development is mediated by—is revealed and accomplished through—socially organized and, often, language-mediated activities (Dyson, 1993). In these activities, the exchange of language among learners in particular social contexts enhances literacy development, which includes interpreting and communicating meaning of written and oral language.

> Literacy is a cultural tool for taking action in the world, and that action is usually derived from an interaction between children and adults.

A Social Constructivist Perspective on Teaching

When looking through a social constructivist lens, we see the teacher as a "guide on the side" as opposed to the "sage on the stage" (Rosenblatt, 1978). Although previous conceptions of teaching and learning emphasized the teacher's role in transmitting knowledge, more recent theories have emphasized the social and interactional nature of learning (Turner & Paris, 1995). The desired relationship between teachers and students (as well as among students) has been described as an apprenticeship in which a more able companion guides, supports, and assists the learner.

Furthermore, since the nature of these interactions with others in the classroom represents different types of apprenticeships, each situation may offer new insights which contribute to the construction of meaning through interaction (Riordan-Karlsson, 1997). This may include sharing authority between the teacher and the students (Ruddell & Unrau, 1994), negotiating meaning among friends, or cooperative learning (Johnson & Johnson, 1975, 1985), creating completely new ideas from a combination of minds.

In the case when a more knowledgeable partner or adult supports the child's performance in various reading and writing activities, the metaphor of a scaffold (Wood, Bruner, & Ross, 1976) is often used. From this perspective, knowledge and understandings are constructed when individuals engage in social conversations and activities about shared problems or tasks. Children in classrooms and home environments encounter these activities, problems, and tasks every day. Social constructivists believe that children learn more when the interaction centers on tasks the students cannot do alone but can do with expert assistance. Vygotsky's (1978) theory of learning claims that these assisted interactions occur within the zone of proximal development (ZPD) which he defines as:

> "The distance between the actual developmental level as determined by independent problem solving and the level of potential development as determined through problem solving under adult guidance or in collaboration with more capable peers" (p. 86).

Concluding Remarks

When children are learning to read and write in our classrooms, we must give them the room to grow, explore, and discover the world around them. As they create stories and pictures to share with others, we are able to see the world through their eyes. They are carving a place for themselves in our literate society, which is an important part of the learning process.

As we embark on our journey through the eyes of an emergent learner, we need to look at how young children attempt to construct knowledge and the important roles reading and writing play in our classrooms. We need to remind ourselves that reading and writing are, in fact, components of the learning process; therefore, we should focus on the process, not the product.

This book will focus mainly on the process of writing, but that, by its nature, includes the reading that takes place during writing. We will discuss emergent literate behaviors in the home environment and in the classroom and ways to integrate reading. Additionally, alternative forms of assessment, which can be used to evaluate children's progress and growth as they embark on a lifelong literacy journey, will be addressed.

When children are learning to read and write in our classrooms, we must give them the room to grow, explore, and discover the world around them.

Reading and Writing Connections

Initial Reading and Writing

When we look at research on the reading and writing connections, the first documented research was as early as 1929; however, most of the research conducted on this connection has occurred between 1970 and the present (DeFord, 1994). The key insights revealed through this body of research discuss the nature of reading and writing as well as the shared knowledge structures which are evident in the two processes (DeFord, 1994).

Both reading and writing involve subroutines or subprocesses (Irwin & Doyle, 1992). Some of these subroutines include recognizing letter formation, the phonological relationships, the use of attention, and the use of memory which is needed to read and write. As readers and writers, children process information on many different levels, which can be difficult for emergent readers and writers. Although it seems as though reading and writing includes a series of steps, the coordination of these particular steps is what makes the process work. Usually, writers create a story according to a series of events they record and illustrate. When retelling a series of events, young writers will often add information which they have forgotten to include because the process is quite difficult. Remembering each subroutine or subprocess can be overwhelming for emergent readers and writers, which may cause frustration.

> As readers and writers, children process information on many different levels, which can be difficult for emergent readers and writers.

The reading and writing processes are interrelated in many respects, including the stages children progress through as well as the instructional practices of teachers. Early reading and writing involves stages that young children progress through at varying rates. These stages include the intention to use the process in a meaningful way, purposes, monitoring the processes in action, searching for useful information, rehearsal strategies, and self-correction, which are all important to the outcomes of both reading and writing (Clay, 1991; Dyson, 1989; Goodman & Goodman, 1979; Harste, Burke, & Woodward, 1984).

On one hand, a proficient reader uses prior knowledge about the linguistic system and the symbolic system and uses these cues to establish expectations and monitor the reading process, as well as comprehend the text. On the other hand, a proficient writer brings the same prior knowledge and experiences to the writing process and uses these sources of information for specific purposes to communicate meaningful messages for him or herself and others. The different strategies that good readers and writers use during this process include predicting, searching, rereading, redrafting, and revising, monitoring and rethinking (Butler & Turnbill, 1984; Clay, 1991; Goodman & Goodman, 1979).

> **Indeed, there is a powerful connection between reading and writing.**

Indeed, there is a powerful connection between reading and writing. It has been found consistently across studies on initial reading and writing that better writers tend to be better readers and that better readers tend to produce more syntactically complex writing than poorer readers (Stotsky, 1983). Often children get ideas for their own stories from reading books and literature or listening as someone else tells a story. Additionally, proficient writers tend to read their stories aloud to an audience more often; therefore, they have the opportunity to practice their oral reading skills, hence the strong connection between reading and writing in a child's world.

Phonemic Awareness

The awareness of the sounds or phonemes that make up spoken words is called phonemic awareness, which is very important for learning to read. "In alphabetic languages, letters (and letter clusters) represent phonemes, and in order to learn the correspondences between letters and sounds, one must have some understanding of the notion that words are made up of phonemes" (Williams, 1995, p. 185). Since phonemes are abstract units, this keen insight is not easily achievable. Although many young children can break words into syllables, phonemic segmentation of a word is very difficult. Studies have concluded that there is a strong correlation between phonemic awareness and reading performance in first and second grades (Williams, 1995). Therefore, teachers can help children acquire phonemic awareness by providing opportunities to practice segmenting words, using games, rhymes, and alliteration. These types of activities can enhance phonics instruction or other reading instruction. Spelling activities and the use of invented spelling are considered to be valuable practice as well. **On the following page is an activity that can be used to practice phonemic awareness with your students.** "Identifying the Beginning, Middle, and Final Sounds in Spoken Words" offers a few songs that will encourage children to listen to the phonemes in the words and concentrate on the beginning, middle, and final sounds of each word. Additional examples may include deleting and substituting phonemes in words and counting phonemes in familiar words.

The reading and writing processes are so intertwined that one cannot happen without the other. They cannot be taught separately; rather, you need to emphasize to your students the connection between reading and writing. From the initial motivation to read and write to the final goal of constructing meaning, the similarities of the reading and writing processes are glaringly obvious. Therefore, it is important to teach our students how these processes are connected and to understand the links among all four literacies—reading, writing, speaking, and listening—which are present in our classrooms every day.

Young children are not afraid to share their writing with others.

Motivation to Read and Write

Increasing students' engagement in reading and writing tasks in the classroom has become a major goal for teachers. No longer is the only goal of reading and writing instruction the "how to," but now the goal is to teach the "want to" as well. Certainly for young children, the motivation is already present. They desperately want to become a participating member of a literate society and "copy" older brothers or sisters and parents. This is evident in children's attempts at making a grocery list to go shopping with a parent or writing a letter to Santa Claus requesting a favorite toy for Christmas. The motivation comes from within the child, which is termed intrinsic motivation. Intrinsic or internal motivation is characterized by a desire to engage in an activity because doing so brings personal satisfaction (Riordan-Karlsson, 1996). When working with young children, it is quite simple to witness their personal satisfaction upon completion of a written story or drawing. Often they ask you to read it, or they offer to read it for you. Sometimes they want you to hang it up on the refrigerator at home or on the bulletin board in the classroom. Of course, now as more and more children are exposed to the technological advances, they may want to "publish" their work on the computer

Young children are not afraid to share their writing with others. However, as children get older they may become fearful of sharing their writing. A hesitance to share one's writing signifies an insecurity of ability or talent. Young authors are not yet aware of grades, cor-

Identifying the Beginning, Middle, and Final Sounds in Spoken Words

Sounds in Songs

Sing songs that encourage children to think about sounds in music. You may choose to emphasize a single sound throughout the song, or each verse may focus on a different sound. Songs can also emphasize medial or final sounds. The following are examples of sound isolation activities.

Sing to the tune of "Old MacDonald Had a Farm."

> What's the sound that starts these words:
> *Turtle, time,* and *teeth*?
> /t/ is the sound that starts these words:
> *Turtle, time,* and *teeth.*
> With a /t/, /t/ here and a /t/, /t/ there,
> Here a /t/, there a /t/, everywhere a /t/, /t/.
> /t/ is the sound that starts these words:
> *Turtle, time,* and *teeth*!
>
> (Yopp, 1992)

Sing to the tune of "Row, Row, Row Your Boat."

Teacher:	In *dog, doll,* and *donkey,* Where do we hear the /d/?
Children:	In *dog, doll,* and *donkey,* We hear it at the first.
Teacher:	In *cat, hat,* and *rabbit,* Where do we hear the /t/?
Children:	In *cat, hat,* and *rabbit,* We hear it at the end.
Teacher:	In *basket* and *monkey,* Where do we hear the /k/?
Children:	In *basket* and *monkey,* We hear it in the middle.

Sing to the tune of "Where Has My Little Dog Gone?"

Teacher:	Where, oh where do you hear the /b/? Where, oh where can it be? In *bird* and *bug* and *bed* and *bark,* Where, oh where can it be?
Children:	At the first.

Reprinted from TCM 2316—Phonics, Phonemic Awareness. . . .

rect spelling, and penmanship, so their inhibitions do not interfere with their efforts to read and write. They are intrinsically motivated to write because of the pure joy it brings to themselves and to others.

Another type of motivation is called extrinsic or external motivation, which is described as something that engages us in an activity when it is clear that by participating in it, we are likely to have a positive experience and accomplish our desired outcome (Riordan-Karlsson, 1996). An example of extrinsic motivation may be receiving a sticker from the teacher on a drawing or a smile from a grandparent when a child delivers a handmade birthday card. As children develop into writers, external motivations become more apparent, such as a concern for perfect spelling or penmanship. Grades and the teacher's approval can quickly become an external motivator for children to write. Developing intrinsic motivation and providing many opportunities and experiences that engage students in meaningful, exciting literacy activities within your classroom should be a goal for every teacher.

Construction of Meaning

A shared goal of both reading and writing is the construction of meaning. For readers, the meaning does not reside solely within the print on the page or the author's intended purpose. Instead, the meaning resides in the reader who reads the print on the page, builds on prior knowledge to form new knowledge, and creates a personal interpretation or meaning of the text. If a reader interacts with other children and shares ideas, then the meaning is constructed as a result of the interactions and the negotiations among the children.

> If a reader interacts with other children and shares ideas, then the meaning is constructed as a result of the interactions and the negotiations among the children.

As authors, children have the power to construct meaning through their stories and illustrations, which allows for readers to construct their own meanings. As children write, new meanings emerge, and with each stroke of the pencil or crayon, a new dimension is added. Sometimes the story a child writes has meaning only for him or her, which is fine. We should not expect to be able to construct meaning from every text that is written by our students, especially since writing is a form of personal expression.

Concluding Remarks

In sum, there are many connections between the reading and writing processes our students engage in each day. Instructional strategies and activities that emphasize this connection for your students will encourage them to integrate the two processes, thus contributing to motivation and comprehension. In both the reading and writing processes there is freedom for different interpretations of meaning, which is encouraged in a social constructivist classroom.

Becoming Young Authors

It is the responsibility
of the teacher to
bridge the gaps among
children's home,
community, and
school experiences
that can be
accomplished through
writing.

Family and Community Influences

The family and community influence is dominant in children's early print experiences that are embedded in socially valued activities. We know that most homes and communities in all economic and social levels, lifestyles, cultures, and ethnicities are filled with language and literacy activities (Heath, 1983; Heller, 1990; Moll, 1994). However, we have learned that we cannot use social categories to predict success in reading and writing (Harste et al., 1984; Sulzby, Teale, & Kamberelis, 1989). Instead, we should acknowledge the diversity of language use and literacy experiences children bring with them to school and understand that learning routines in school may not always match learning routines found in the homes of our students. It is the responsibility of the teacher to bridge the gaps among children's home, community, and school experiences that can be accomplished through writing. Children and parents can also fill this gap with classroom visits from parents or presentations on cultural traditions observed at home. If another language is spoken at home, perhaps the presentation can be on literacy activities the child is involved with at home or with other family members. Displays of written language in the forms of personal letters, cards, or notes can help other children understand the differences in letters and sounds used in other languages, which can be an interesting phonemic awareness activity.

Young authors begin their careers at home with their families as their first audiences; therefore, the family influence can be empowering to a child. Each time a child picks up a pencil, pen, crayon, or marker and writes his or her thoughts, ideas, images, or messages on a piece of paper, an author is born and reborn. Celebrate with children when they bring messages or writings from home; because they will learn that there is a valuable connection between the literacy activities they engage in at home and those they engage in at school. This connection can make a difference in the successful careers of young authors as they progress through their lifelong literacy journeys.

Early Writing

Writing can be viewed as a continuum of growth with each different type of writing behavior and pattern falling somewhere on that continuum. Similar to the early stages of reading development, children begin writing before they enter into school for formal instruction. Usually, early writing does not resemble what we consider conventional writing; however, the young author believes it to be just perfect. For years, early writing has been called "scribbling" or drawings, but in actuality it is rule-governed, organized, and orderly, similar to conventional writing (Ruddell & Ruddell, 1995). The scribbles or random markings on paper are sometimes called "scribble writing" or "pretend writing." This designates the phase of early writing when the written form of the scribbles does not look like standard English orthography even though some children's scribbles are in a long wavy format that resembles cursive writing. Today, with the focus on emergent literacy, we should not ignore scribble writing or random marks on the paper. Scribble writing has achieved a place in our classrooms, either in the writing centers, on bulletin boards, or in the library. It is considered to be true writing when it is read by the author and will gradually resemble more conventional writing as children explore and discover the rules and structures of the conventional written language used by older children and adults.

Current Understandings About Children's Writing Development

Our broadening knowledge base of early writing and how writers develop now serves as a foundation for classroom practice (Dyson & Freedman, 1991). In the following discussion, examples of children's writing illustrate current understandings about children's writing development as summarized by researcher Lesley Morrow (1993, pp. 234–237) who has spent many hours with beginning writers.

> Young authors begin their careers at home with their families as their first audiences; therefore, the family influence can be empowering to a child.

"As a process, early writing development is characterized by children's moving from playfully making marks on paper, through communicating messages on paper, to making texts as artifacts" (Morrow, 1993, pp. 234).

Harste et al. (1984) found that young writers have the ability to distinguish between art and writing as in three-year-old Mary Kate's example in Figure 1.

Figure 1—Mary Kate's picture

Though the picture is small and the explanation is brief, the piece carries a story unique to the characters and holds significance to the author.

When asked about her picture, Mary Kate explained:

> It is me and Madeline (her best friend) playing dress-up...see? And that's my name, Mary Kate, up there.

Clearly, this is a work of art which is one way a child can represent meaning and understanding of his or her place in the world. Mary Kate expresses the importance of playing dress-up with her best friend, Madeline, by drawing a picture. She feels it is important enough to record the event on a piece of paper to share with others. Though the picture is small and the explanation is brief, the piece carries a story unique to the characters and holds significance for the author. Lucy Calkins (1994) believes that significance cannot be found; it must be grown. It is grown in each piece of writing when a child records one of life's stories. Writing is the process of making significance of life's events.

On the top of the picture, where Mary Kate attempts to spell her name, she is expressing pride in her authorship. She knows there is an "M" in her name as well as some other letters, so she tries her best to write her name so others will know it is her story and her piece of art.

In another example in Figure 2, Mary Kate drew a picture of her mother going to work and once again attempted to write her name to claim ownership of her piece of writing.

Figure 2

Mary Kate draws pictures of significant people in her life and the world around her.

Mary Kate draws pictures of significant people in her life and the world around her. She uses writing and artwork as a way of expressing her love and appreciation of her family and friends. Each time she draws a picture, she is telling a new story, and then she reads aloud the story that accompanies the drawing. It is evident that Mary Kate is in the early stage of writing as she draws symbols to represent her story. Although she does not know her sound-letter correspondence, she is confident that her idea is significant enough to make it into a picture and sign her name as the author. Her eagerness to express her ideas and her knowledge of writing are apparent in her drawings. She uses writing patterns in an individualistic way while on her way to becoming a conventional writer.

Form and Function

"Children learn the uses of written language before they learn the forms" (Morrow, 1993, p. 235). Four-year-old Patrick writes his Christmas list in Figure 3. This is an important event for him, and he wants to express what he wants from Santa. He feels the best way to accomplish this is by writing it down. He is familiar with this particular function of writing, yet he has not yet learned the correct form. Patrick wants costumes, a glove, and a musical instrument, such as a tuba, flute, violin, or drum. Children practice writing excitedly when writing serves a useful purpose in their lives. Patrick's Christmas list clearly illustrates this.

Six-year-old Meghan writes in her journal every day about important events in her life, such as her birthday, her trip to New York City to see *The Lion King,* and when her cousin came to visit her. Meghan's journal entries are evidence that form follows function in beginning writing. In this particular journal entry, Meghan weaves in her connections to characters from a favorite book.

> *On Fiday I went to Noyoc to sey the Chismitey.*
>
> *And I wet to a toy sor.*
>
> *And I wet to the plis wer elwes lev.*
>
> *Then I wen to stetpati*

(Translation: On Friday I went to New York to see the Christmas tree. And I went to a toy store. And I went to The Plaza where Eloise lives. Then I went to St. Patrick's.)

Meghan's busy trip to New York City was important to her, especially her visit to The Plaza to see if Eloise was there. Meghan's interest in Eloise stems from repeated readings of the book *Eloise* by Kay Thompson.

Figure 3

Figure 4

Meghan

Decemb 8. 1997

On Fiday I
went to Noyoc
to sey the
Chismitey. And
I wet to a
toyzor. And I

Figure 4 *(cont.)*

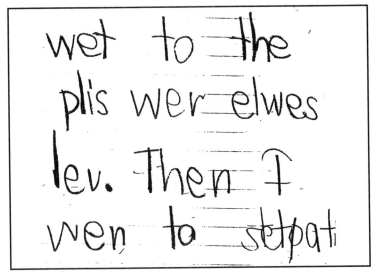

wet to the
plis wer elwes
lev. Then T
wen to setpati

Many of Meghan's journal entries are important events in her life that she wants to share and make public; therefore, she writes them in her journal and reads them to her class during share time. She is planting seeds for her stories and creating memories or memoirs that will be a reflection of her life and who she is. Meghan is the oldest of her cousins; therefore, she feels a responsibility to be a good role model. Many of her journal entries and subsequent stories are about her cousins as seen in Figures 5 and 5a.

Many of Meghan's journal entries are important events in her life that she wants to share and make public; therefore, she writes them in her journal and reads them to her class during share time.

> *In Febueree my cosin Luki wil be one. He cen woc but he needs som help. I wish that I cod be with hem.*
>
> *Happ Brthday*

(Translation: In February my cousin Lukas will be one. He can walk but he needs some help. I wish that I could be with him. Happy Birthday.)

> *On Towsday my mom towd me that I had A bebey cosit hrr nem is Colen.*

(Translation: On Tuesday my mom told me that I had a baby cousin. Her name is Colleen.)

It is clear Meghan understands that her journal is a place to record her thoughts, ideas, daily events, and auspicious occasions. She also enjoys drawing pictures to accompany her journal entries, which then become longer stories. Meghan knows her alphabet and phonetically spells her words. It is evident in her writing that she knows her letter-sound correspondence, how to write a sentence, and that the beginning letter of a sentence should be capitalized.

Figure 5

Meghan
January 22, 1991
In Febueree
my cosin Luki
wil be one.
He cen woc
but he needs
som help.

I wish that
I cod be with
hem.

Happ Brthday

Meghan
January 15 1998
On Towsday
my mom towd
me that I had
A bebey Casit
hrr nem is Colen.

She demonstrates her growing command of conventional written language forms and, additionally, her understanding that titles, capital letters, and punctuation have functions to serve in written text.

The act of writing plays an important role in Meghan's life. When asked about her writing experiences, Meghan explains, "I love to write and draw pictures because it is fun. Me and my friends like to write stories." She also understands that writing is a form of communication, as evidenced in her thank you note (Figure 6) to her cousin. She has seen her mother write thank you notes and has received them herself; therefore, she understands that writing messages is a socially valued activity.

> *Dear Lukas,*
>
> *Thanks for coming to my house.*
>
> *Love*
>
> *Meghan*

Although Meghan knows that neither Mary Kate nor Patrick are fluent readers, she writes directions for them and leaves the messages hanging on the front door so they will see them there.

In another example of purposeful writing in Figure 7, Meghan leaves a message for her four-year-old cousin, Patrick, and her three-year-old sister, Mary Kate, as to where they can find surprises. She communicates directions for them, using text and arrows, on a Post-it note and hangs it on the door at their eye level.

> *Mary Kate go riyf necst to mommy then stop owkiy*

(Translation: Mary Kate go right next to mommy then stop okay.)

> *Pat keyp on gooing streyd and then trn and go ststeyt*

(Translation: Pat keep on going straight and then turn and go straight.)

Although Meghan knows that neither Mary Kate nor Patrick is a fluent reader, she writes directions for them and leaves the messages hanging on the front door so they will see them there. She has witnessed adults leaving written messages for others, so she internalizes this purpose and assimilates it into a familiar context to meet her purpose.

These examples of young authors using written text as a way of sharing ideas, communicating messages, and recording significant events illustrate the miracles of literacy in our daily lives. Young children are constantly trying to make sense of the world around them, and it is through writing that they can explore their world. While engaged in a variety of literacy activities, they become participatory members in our society and feel a sense of belonging. As children grow and develop into young authors, each step in their literacy journey warrants praise and celebration.

Inventions and Reinventions

"Children's writing develops through constant invention and reinvention of the forms of written language" (Morrow, 1993, p. 236). A number of principles children discover about writing forms have been identified by researcher Marie Clay (1975); they include the recurring principle, the generative principle, and the flexibility principle. The recurring principle explains how writing consists of recurring figures and moves, such as the rounded, curved, and straight lines children use in their writing. The generative principle is the idea that children can generate an unlimited number of words from a limited number of letter combinations. And the flexibility principle claims that the same letters can be written in different ways, such as cursive and upper and lowercase; however, there are limits as to the acceptability of letter reconfiguration and permutation, such as "b" and "d" but not "c" (Ruddell & Ruddell, 1995).

As children invent and reinvent written language forms, they discover these principles; recall Mary Kate's repeated attempts to write her name. Children move from nonconventional to conventional written forms through the process of discovering conventional forms of writing, i.e., inventing and reinventing written forms (Temple, Nathan, Temple, & Burris, 1993). It is throughout this process that children construct theories and test their hypotheses about the conventional written language system (Ruddell & Ruddell, 1994).

Furthermore, recent research has found that "as children move from nonconventional to conventional written language, they individually and separately make essentially the same discoveries about written language in essentially the same order" (Temple et al., 1993, p.2).

When observing children who exhibit similar writing patterns in your classroom, you need to understand that children use individualistic ways to learn the same principles. Keep in mind that the writing patterns that a child exhibits at a given time only reflect the hypothesis about written language the child is testing at that time. It does not reflect other knowledge the child may have about writing or indicate any strengths or weaknesses in his or her overall literacy development.

Figure 6

Dear Lukas,

Thanks for coming to my house.

Love
Meghan

Figure 7

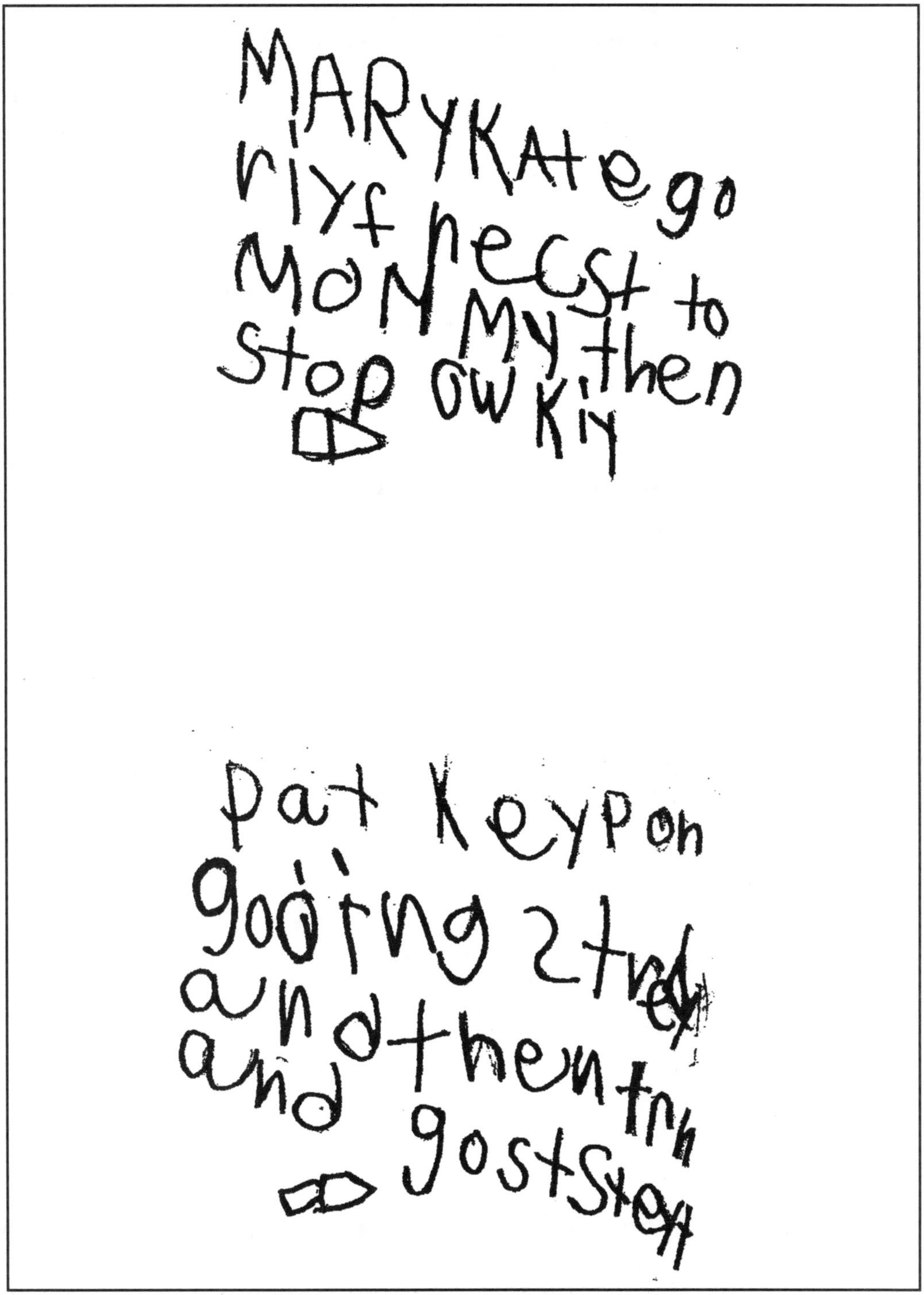

MARYKATego
rlyf necst to
MONMy then
stop ow kiy

pat Keypon
gooing 2trd
and thentrn
and gost ste ff

25

Invented Spelling

As children gain control over the spelling rules of the English language, they use invented spelling as they progress toward conventional spelling. Researchers Temple and Gillet (1989) have identified patterns of invented spelling development. The first pattern is *prephonemic spelling,* which is made up of letter and letter-like forms. The writer indicates awareness that a combination of letters forms a word written in a horizontal line. This is typical of writers in kindergarten and first grade. Recall Mary Kate's attempts at writing her name with her pictures.

Early phonemic spelling is the second pattern identified in invented spelling development. This pattern consists of letters and letter-like forms in short consonant strings, indicating that the writer is aware of the alphabetic principle. This is also typical of writers in kindergarten, first graders, and beginning readers; recall Patrick's Christmas list.

The third pattern is *letter-name spelling* in which names are used to represent sounds in words; for example, the name "aich" is used to represent the letter "h" because it is the only letter in the alphabet with the "ch" sound in its name (Ruddell & Ruddell, 1995). This pattern indicates that the writer has a clear awareness of a symbol-sound relationship without understanding the relationship completely.

This pattern is illustrated in Figure 7 (Meghan's notes to Patrick and Mary Kate on page 25) and is typical of beginning readers, most first graders, and many second graders.

Transitional spelling is the fourth pattern, the one in which letters are used to represent all sounds. This is typical of more advanced readers. This pattern reveals that the writer almost completely understands the spelling system by correctly representing long and short vowel sounds.

Pattern five is called *derivational spelling*; letters are used to reflect spelling patterns for vowel marking and consonant doubling that are rule-governed. Derivational spelling patterns show a lack of awareness of the relational patterns in words derived from the same base as is seen in more mature spelling (Ruddell & Ruddell, 1995).

This pattern is typical of children and adults who have exhibited some fluency but who have not read extensively.

In order to better understand children's spelling progress and their growth in representing words in written forms, we can use these patterns as guidelines. Although movement through these patterns can

> As children gain control over the spelling rules of the English language, they use invented spelling as they progress toward conventional spelling.

move back and forth among patterns and can exhibit elements of more than one pattern at a time. Therefore, use these patterns as guidelines, not standards.

It is important to encourage children to use invented spelling so they do not spend needless amounts of time and worry over spelling every word correctly. In time, as children progress as writers and readers, spelling patterns and rules will be learned. There is no need to place any extra pressure on young authors. There is a strong connection between invented spelling and phonemic awareness; therefore, encouragement of invented spelling is beneficial to all children, especially those who need assistance with literacy acquisition.

When children ask for assistance in spelling a word, the first inclination is to spell it for them or have them sound it out. Instead, ask the student to visualize the word while sounding it out. Help them to realize that they have resources other than an adult to draw upon. Invite your students to say the word slowly and stretch it out and listen to the sounds. Remind them also to think of how a word looks once it is written, not only of how it sounds. Sometimes children will remember how a word looks without knowing each letter and the correct order.

Concluding Remarks

It is important that children use writing in authentic meaningful ways, either to express ideas or communicate. Writing is a commitment to inquiry, a process of recording information, facts, and ideas and then developing them into stories to share with others. Many of our children's stories may be brief but filled with layers of meanings, and the meanings emerge as children read and share their stories. When children are immersed in writing for personal reasons, the process is more enjoyable, and the product is worthy of praise from others, which builds self-confidence. Unfortunately, in many classrooms, writing is seen as a chore (writing answers to reading comprehension questions) or a punishment (writing a misspelled word ten times). If writing is perceived as an enjoyable, creative activity, many children will eagerly engage in the act of writing and produce beautiful pieces. Moreover, if young authors are personally involved in their own writing, teachers do not have to think of one hundred ways to motivate them to write. Therein lies a lesson for all teachers.

> **It is important to encourage children to use invented spelling so they do not spend needless amounts of time and worry over spelling every word correctly.**

Literacy Activities at Home

Parents, grandparents, and siblings play a critical role in children's early literacy development by promoting literacy in the home environment and providing the appropriate materials, books, paper, pencils, crayons, and magazines.

Family Literacy

The literacy activities in the home environment will vary according to socioeconomic status and cultural background. Most of the literacy events that occur in the sociocultural context of the home environment involve social interactions and conversations, which greatly influence emergent readers and writers.

Contributions of family literacy practices are a new field of investigation that extends beyond the limits I have set forth in this book; therefore, I will be focusing only on a few reading and writing practices that are contributions from family literacy practices. Parents, grandparents, and siblings play a critical role in children's early literacy development by promoting literacy in the home environment and providing the appropriate materials, books, paper, pencils, crayons, and magazines. Additionally, they often give help and instructions and emphasize the value of literacy. In many instances, adults in the home not only provide opportunities and materials but also reasons for reading and writing, which instill a desire and motivation in the child to master the skills needed to read and write and become a literate member of society.

In the home environment there are several purposeful engagements in literacy events. Through daily conversations, a child learns how to adopt a social voice in a context where multiple voices are heard. Additionally, the opportunities to connect past experiences with new experiences to reconstruct knowledge through communication are plentiful. The following activities illustrate many wonderful ways that children engage in literacy in the home environment.

Storybook Reading

Storybook reading is one of the most popular and valued reading activities a parent and child can enjoy together. Many research studies of parent-child storybook reading (Bloome, 1985; Heath, 1983; Ninio & Bruner, 1978; Teale & Sulzby, 1987) and of classroom storybook reading (Cochran-Smith, 1984; Green & Harker, 1982; Martinez & Teale, 1987) conclude that the act of reading books aloud to a child is characteristically a socially created activity. In the situations and cultures studied, children almost never encounter solely an oral rendering of the text of the book in a storybook reading situation. Instead, the words of the author are spoken by the adult reader and heard by the children who are listening. During storybook reading, it is common for the reader and the listener to exchange questions, answers, ideas, and interpretations of the story.

Storybook reading confirms that reading books aloud to children is fundamentally an act of social construction of knowledge and ideas.

Storybook reading confirms that reading books aloud to children is fundamentally an act of social construction of knowledge and ideas. The language and social interaction that surround the text are critical to the nature of this construction; in fact, they appear to be good candidates for what makes storybook reading so powerful an influence in young children's literacy development (Sulzby & Teale, 1985).

> "Children take great pleasure in being read to; this is clear from the frequency and persistence with which they ask adults to read to them. It seems that children can be introduced to books at various ages and that they can develop strong, positive feelings about books and being read to, especially when the reading is embedded in relationships with people who are important to them" (McLane & McNamee, 1990, p. 74).

Children can learn that the print on a page and the words in a story are permanent. No matter who reads the story, a parent, teacher, or caregiver, or where the story is read, at home or in school, the words of the story stay the same. Although the words may be the same, the meaning can be negotiated between the participants in the reading event.

Also, through storybook reading and storytelling, children learn story structure. They learn that most of their favorite stories, especially fairy tales, begin with "Once upon a time..." and conclude with

"...and they lived happily ever after." The elements of the story are important for a child to learn, that there is a beginning, middle, and an end to each story and that there are a villain and a hero (a bad person and a good person). Children will also learn that there is a problem or conflict that is described and then resolved with a happy ending. When children begin to tell their own versions of the story, they usually begin with "Once upon a time..." and end with "and they lived happily ever after." The middle section is usually the improvised story or, in many cases, a personalized version of the old fairy tale.

Making Stories Part of a Child's World

The following example comes from an informal observation of a child learning the complexities of story structure. In a long car ride home, Meghan was telling her mother her story about Cinderella.

> "Once upon a time there was a girl named Cinderella, and she had two mean stepsisters, Drizzela and Anastesia. And they were going to the ball and her mean stepmother said, 'No you can't go, Cinderella, you have to stay home and clean the dishes, scrub the floor, and don't forget the laundry!' Then the fairy godmother came and gave Cinderella a dress and turned the pumpkin into a coach. On the way to the ball, she stopped at the A & P (grocery store) to get a snack. She got M& M's, and then she went to the ball...and the slipper fit Cinderella, and they lived happily ever after."

Through her rendition, she aims to follow the story structure she is familiar with, while slightly altering the content of the story according to her own experiences, thus constructing new meanings and reconceptualizing new ideas of the story.

This is Meghan's personal rendition of the classic fairy tale, *Cinderella;* however, she decided to add a detour for Cinderella so she would not be hungry when she went to the ball. Through her rendition, she aims to follow the story structure she is familiar with while slightly altering the content of the story according to her own experiences, thus constructing new meanings and reconceptualizing new ideas of the story. She is able to do this after participating in repeated readings of this favorite story and repeated discussions with her parents.

In the following example, Meghan is "reading" the story of *The Nutcracker Suite* to her six-months-old sister after repeated readings with her parents. She carefully turns the pages and points to the brilliant pictures.

> "The Nutcracker (reads the front cover and then turns to the first page). Okay, this is a story about a little girl, Maria, and she gets this present from her uncle for Christmas. It is a nutcracker. And then this is the Sugar Plum Fairy that dances around and takes her to the land of sweets. See all of the candy? And these are the dancing bears. And then the nutcracker saves her. The end! Wasn't that a nice story?"

Meghan is imitating her parents when they read stories to her. She has learned how to participate in the storybook reading activity, and she is initiating her younger sister into the literate environment in their home. **On the following page is an extension activity that can be used in a fairy tale unit.** A discussion about the setting of a story is an important pre-reading activity. This activity encourages children to think about the settings of some favorite fairy tales, such as *Little Red Riding Hood, The Little Mermaid,* and *Rapunzel.*

Instilling a Love of Reading

The invaluable insights that children learn from being read to can play a prominent role when they go to school and begin formal reading and writing instruction. Reading books to children, whether at home or in childcare settings, helps them connect their personal worlds with the larger social worlds they live in—the family world, the school world, or the neighborhood and community world. It is also a way to instill in children a love of reading and an enjoyment of stories that can last a lifetime. Their amusement and satisfaction gained from storybook reading can motivate them to learn the more technical aspects of reading, such as decoding print and phonemic awareness, which are necessary for learning to read, and the technical aspects of writing, such as word formation, sentence structure, and character development. The interaction that occurs through an activity such as storybook reading clearly influences a child's reading development in many ways.

> Reading books to children, whether at home or in childcare settings, helps them connect their personal worlds with the larger social worlds they live in—the family world, the school world, or the neighborhood and community world.

Vygotsky (1978) considers this interaction to be critical within the zone of proximal development. With the assistance of an adult, a child can reach the level of potential development while engaged in storybook reading activities.

Storybook reading also illustrates Vygotsky's (1978) notion that prior to children solving problems on their own, they first seek guidance from adults or more capable peers. The problem is the fact that they cannot read the print on the page; thus, they need someone to read the story to them, which is their solution. However, over time and with practice, children will internalize the process and learn to read as a result of the interaction in this cherished activity.

Storytelling

Storytelling is an extension of storybook reading and is another contribution from family literacy practices that occurs in the home environment. The oral tradition of storytelling is valued in many cultures in which children like to share with one another. This, too, is an activity that involves social interaction between an adult and a child involved in sharing ideas, knowledge, and experiences. Many cultures value stories of the past and want to pass them on to the next generation.

MATCH THE SETTINGS

The setting of a story is **where** you find the characters.   Here are some characters from stories you have probably heard or read.

Draw a line to match the characters with the settings in which you would find them.

1. Little Red Riding Hood

A castle

2. Charlotte

A forest

3. Aladdin

A tower

4. The Little Mermaid

A farm

5. Beauty

An underground cave

6. Rapunzel

Under the sea

Reprinted from TCM 147—Activities for any Literature Unit—Primary

The contents and the structures of these stories may differ, as well as the interactional patterns, but the goal remains the same—for the storyteller to use both verbal and nonverbal actions to mesmerize the listener and become one of the characters in the story. As Jacobs (1965) emphasizes, a good storyteller enters into the story, lives in it, and in effect loses him or herself in the story and holds the listeners by concealing the story resolution until the very end.

Many ideas for the stories come from previously read storybooks and family stories that are shared at special occasions, for example, holidays, birthdays, and family reunions. In her landmark study on language development, Shirley Brice Heath (1983) studied two communities in the Piedmont area of the Carolinas. She found that in both communities, Roadville (a white working-class community) and Trackton (a black working-class community), families spent a lot of time telling stories, but the forms, contents, and occasions differed greatly. "One community allows only stories which are factual and have a little exaggeration; the other uses reality only as the germ of a highly creative fictionalized account. One uses stories to reaffirm group membership and behavioral norms, the other to assert individual strengths and powers" (p. 184). As a result, she reported that the children in the two communities heard different kinds of stories and developed competence in telling stories in highly contrasting ways.

> The social interactions and dialogues surrounding the activity of storytelling resonate in the community, which leads children to tell their own stories to peers, siblings, and parents.

Most importantly, storytelling provides a forum for oral traditions to be explored, thus merging with literate traditions which also influence learning to read and write. The social interactions and dialogues surrounding the activity of storytelling resonate in the community, which leads children to tell their own stories to peers, siblings, and parents. This is a form of weaving in personal experiences and making interconnections with literacy events. The tradition of storytelling is passed on from generation to generation, thus introducing the children to a symbolic world through the guidance of the vicars of their culture (Bruner, 1986) and teaching the children how to understand their world. These stories teach the morals of the cultural group to the younger generation.

Role-Playing

Fantasy playing or dramatization with characters and plots from a story is a favorite activity for young children who have been read to. This activity illustrates the metaphor Vygotsky (1978) uses, the buds or flowers that, with assistance, will "fruit" into independent accomplishments. After being read to by an adult, the child may choose to carry out the activity independently and then pretend to be the teacher and read to dolls or stuffed animals or younger siblings, or they may integrate written letters or greeting cards into their play. From an early age, reading can serve as a form of communication and as a connection to children's social world, especially through role-playing and dramatization. **On the following page is an activity on dramatization that can get children involved in the stories they read.** This can improve their reading and writing skills.

This "pretend" fantasy playing takes children one step closer to actual reading; therefore, those children who have been read to understand some fundamentals of reading. They are familiar with reading strategies, such as looking at the pictures for context clues and understanding that the words on the page are a message or a form of communication. Story structure is learned; the idea that there is a beginning, middle, and an end to each story and development of a sight vocabulary, such as recognizing the word "cat" from *The Cat in The Hat* story, are all positive results of reading to children.

Young children often role-play as teacher and students and use literacy events as the focus of their play. Or sometimes children will role-play a writing piece and assign their siblings or friends to be the characters. Either way, children are learning through role-play when they take new perspectives on everyday happenings, such as going to the store or playing a game with a brother or sister. It is the daily occurrences that children write about in their stories.

Writing Activities

Since young children have a natural desire to tell stories and talk about things they have seen, this is a wonderful opportunity for you to encourage them to develop a sense of observing and writing.

Since young children have a natural desire to tell stories and talk about things they have seen, this is a wonderful opportunity for you to encourage them to develop a sense of observing and writing. Every simple activity that parents and children engage in, be it reading a story or doing a puzzle, contributes to the knowledge base inside a young child's head.

Early exposure and experience with print in the home includes reading aloud the daily weather report from the newspaper or writing a grocery list before going shopping. Other activities, such as making birthday cards for friends and relatives or writing a note to a spouse, exhibit literate behavior that young children observe and ultimately imitate. Writing thank you notes is a wonderful writing activity that they can do both at home and in school.

On page 37 is an activity that requires children to compose a thank you note. This form of writing should be a meaningful activity for your students since there is always someone they can send a thank you note to. Additional writing activities related to thank you notes include invitations and friendly letters.

DRAMATIZATION

Dramatizing a story is not only fun for children, but it can greatly improve their reading skills.

Stick Puppets

Materials: white tagboard, paper, craft sticks or straws, scissors, tape or glue

To prepare:

1. Ask the children to name the characters and objects that play important parts in their stories.

2. Have them draw and color the characters on white paper. They may create their own designs or use the outlines of the figures. Some characters may need more than one shape.

3. Help them mount their figures on tagboard and secure them to the ends of craft sticks or straws.

To proceed:

- Children are usually very comfortable projecting their ideas through puppets.

- Initially, the puppets may be used to **teach character traits or actions**. As the teacher makes statements about the characters, children can hold up the correct puppets.

The children's creativity will quickly take over.

- They can experiment with the puppets, **retelling the story** in their own words.

- They can be innovative by **adding new situations** to the story.

- They can use their books and practice **recognizing dialogue** as they read the character parts aloud.

- They can even use their puppets in **presenting a TV commercial** for their books.

Optional:

- Dramatization of a story can be done as a small group or whole class activity. The class can be divided into small groups to **prepare assigned scenes** from a story. One child can be the narrator, reading from the book as the others operate their puppets.

Reprinted from TCM 147—Activities for any Literature Unit—Primary

The Family Journal

Participating in literacy events as a member of the family is very important to emergent readers and writers. Even simple activities that families do become significant events to young children, such as going to the store or picking up the mail. Keeping a family journal is a great idea for parents to record the important family events.

Similar to a writer's notebook, the family journal can include photos, poems, songs, cards, and other items that hold importance for the family members. This is an authentic purpose of literacy that is important for parents to model to their children. Events, occasions, and traditions are worth writing down and remembering. These events are the ones that children usually want to write about and share with their friends.

Parents, grandparents, and children enjoy family journals. Each family member can contribute to the family journal whenever he or she wants to. One night each week may be designated as the "journal night" which is when the family gathers together and discusses an important entry for the journal. Encouraging each member of the family to participate emphasizes the importance of the recording of special events. The value placed on each event will remain with young children for a long time to come.

> Participating in literacy events as a member of the family is very important to emergent readers and writers.

Concluding Remarks

In sum, early exposure and experience with print in the home environment, being read to, seeing adults read, and playing with reading and writing, can assist and prepare a child for formal reading and writing instruction in the school setting. Parents, grandparents, and other literate adults influence the development of literacy by acting as models of literate activities. Children try to imitate their role models engaged in reading and writing activities. Some parents also participate in various literacy activities with their children, which sends a positive message that these literacy activities are indeed very important and valued in the social world in which they live. Some examples of these activities include reading aloud to a child, role-playing a character during their child's "pretend" play or fantasy play, writing stories with their children, or drawing pictures, among other activities.

The Thank You Note: Individual

Activity:

Each student will compose a thank you note.

Materials:

- overhead projector, transparency, and markers
- chart paper and marking pen
- notepaper
- pencils
- crayons, colored pencils, or markers (optional)
- envelopes
- postage

Preparation:

1. Prepare an overhead transparency of the writing paper the children will use.
2. Have each student bring in the name and address of someone to whom to write a thank you note.

Directions:

Ask each child to select an individual for whom it would be appropriate to write a thank you note. Have the children brainstorm ideas that could be included in their thank you notes. Record their responses on chart paper.

Give the children a word bank of names such as grandma, grandpa, aunt, uncle, Mr. _____, Mrs. _____, Mom, Dad, and so forth. This will help them with their future letter writing, as well.

Model for the class the writing of a thank you note. Use the overhead transparency of the same writing paper they will use for their notes.

Next, allow the children to compose their own thank you notes, using the ideas from the chart paper and the overhead transparency to guide them. The note should include a heading, a greeting, a sentence in the body that states that for which the writer is thankful (as well as expressing his or her gratitude), a closing, and the writer's signature. A picture related to the body of the note can be added, if desired.

All thank you notes should be placed in envelopes, addressed, stamped, and mailed. However, if all the notes are written to the same person, they can be placed in one envelope and mailed together, or if the notes are addressed to the students' parents, allow them to draw stamps on their envelopes and hand-deliver their letters.

Reprinted from TCM 2009—Writing Workshop Lessons . . . : Grades K–3

Writing in the Classroom

A Literacy-Rich Classroom

> The goal, of course, is to create a classroom in which children understand the value of literacy.

When you walk into a literacy-rich classroom, you see letters and numbers all over the room, correct? This is only half of the definition of a literacy-rich classroom. The other half involves providing opportunities for children to engage in literacy activities throughout the day in a variety of ways. The goal, of course, is to create a classroom in which children understand the value of literacy. There is no perfect recipe for a literacy-rich classroom since it is the combination of literacy materials, rituals, and activities designed to interact with print as well as with other sources in meaningful ways. Some of the items that should be included in a literacy-rich classroom include charts, books, alphabets, paper and pencil, labels, pictures, and a class notebook for ideas, photos, and souvenirs from field trips. This class notebook can be a source of writing ideas for your students.

In a literacy-rich classroom, materials are available for every child, and there is a sufficient amount of time devoted to engagement in various activities throughout the day. Reading and writing are integrated with activities and tasks even during playtime. Literacy is so deeply embedded into the fabric of the classroom, it is difficult to separate it out. For example, there may be a pad of paper next to the telephone in the housekeeping corner, or a list of shapes and colors in the block area, or a cash register and receipts in the grocery store. These are all wonderful examples of authentic literacy activities.

The most natural places you will find evidence of reading and writing in a literacy-rich classroom include the library, the writing center, and the publishing center. In many early childhood classrooms, children flock to these areas during playtime since they view many literacy activities as "play." It is not until the first grade that these activities become "work." Therefore, you need to capitalize on your students' excitement and motivation to read and write whenever you can. If you ask children to engage in a writing activity, do not make it too difficult. Keep it simple, such as, "Can you write a story for me?" or "Do you want to write a card for your mother?" It is important that you do not set high expectations for the young authors in your classroom. If children do not want to write because they think they cannot spell correctly, assure them that it does not matter. Even if a child wants to scribble, encourage him or her to read the story to you so he or she knows you are interested. A caring teacher is one who is more interested in his or her students than in the textbook. Listening to your students and learning from your students are two of the most important qualities of a good teacher. Through various literacy activities you will be afforded the opportunities to both listen and learn right in your very own classroom.

> A display of children's work that is woven into the fabric of the classroom will guide children in their lifelong literacy journeys.

Of course, in a literacy-rich classroom you will see children's writing hung up on the walls, on a clothesline across the room, on closet doors, and on bulletin boards. Why keep it in a folder or a drawer when it can be on display for others to enjoy it? If children are immersed in a literacy-rich classroom, they will value literacy in a unique way. They will see that literacy is not "work" but rather a part of daily life and routines. Think about what a literacy-poor classroom might look like—very sterile with only desks, chairs, and a blackboard. If we want our students to value literacy and engage in multiple literacy activities and rituals, we need to provide the opportunities for them. A display of children's work that is woven into the fabric of the classroom will guide children in their lifelong literacy journeys.

Writing Workshop

It is imperative that you provide a variety of writing opportunities and experiences for your students in your classroom. There are many different teaching practices to guide students' writing, which have been revolutionized due in part to teachers' participation in National Writing Project programs that have helped teachers evolve into writers. The implementation of Writing Project practices is a result of the combination of teachers' awareness of their own power as writers and the integrated view of the reading and writing processes. One of the most popular Writing Project practices which has been implemented in many classrooms is the writing workshop.

Writing workshop describes writing instruction in which a specified period of class time is devoted to children immersed in the act of writing each day (Atwell, 1987; Calkins, 1986, 1991; Graves, 1983).

Writing workshop is an instructional strategy that can begin in kindergarten and extend throughout the elementary grades. The focus is primarily on process rather than product. A goal of writing workshop is for students to have many opportunities to engage in the act of writing and have the autonomy to decide their writing topics and styles. Children also make important decisions about editing and publishing. Nancie Atwell (1987) identifies seven principles that lay the foundation for writing workshop.

> **A goal of writing workshop is for students to have many opportunities to engage in the act of writing and have the autonomy to decide their writing topics and styles.**

Writers need regular chunks of time to brainstorm, read, revise, share, and change their ideas. Writers need to count on time each day to devote to their writing. Writers need to practice writing to be good writers.

Writers need their own topics. A sense of autonomy is a powerful tool for writers. Young authors take pride in writing stories from their own ideas. Writing allows children to express their ideas and determine their social status among family and peers.

Writers need response. Throughout the process of writing, response from peers and teachers is helpful. Questions from friends and adults help the writer rethink ideas and reflect on his or her writing.

Writers learn mechanics in context, not out of context. As corrections and revisions are made to a piece of writing, writers learn the rules and forms of written language in a meaningful context.

Children need to know adults who write. You need to write with your class and share your drafts so they can see what experienced writers go through while composing.

Writers need to read. Children need to be exposed to a variety of genres—prose, poetry, mystery, and autobiography—to learn about writing styles.

Writing teachers need to take responsibility for their knowledge and teaching. You need to utilize professional resources that reflect recent research on children's writing. You need to become a writer and a researcher so you can observe and learn from your own writing and the writing that is produced in your classrooms.

These seven principles can be woven into writing workshop classrooms quite easily. A block of time should be set aside each day for writing workshop, preferably the same time of day so the children understand that writing is part of their daily routine. A regular and dependable schedule is beneficial to all. Children can anticipate writing their stories or sharing their thoughts and ideas with their classmates each day. They learn that writing is a valued activity, and they do not feel rushed to finish their stories in one sitting. The block of time needs to be long enough so children can think of ideas, plan, brainstorm, discuss ideas with peers, revise, rethink, and engage in writing activities without an imposed deadline. Setting aside a block of time devoted to writing creates an environment that invites children to write, similar to professional writers. Virtually every author's reflection on his or her own writing includes the message that to be a writer, one must "write every day" (Briggs, 1991). Therefore, it is important that you create a classroom learning environment that encourages children to become a member of the community of writers that exists in your classroom.

> Virtually every author's reflection on his or her own writing includes the message that to be a writer, one must "write every day" (Briggs, 1991).

Since time is a valuable commodity during the school day, it is wise to integrate reading, spelling, and language arts time into your writing workshop time. It is easier to discuss spelling rules in the context of a student's writing rather than as an abstract rule. You can also plan for a reading-writing workshop that includes children reading their stories to the class or you reading a story to the class to generate topic ideas. Or you may want to combine the writing workshop with project- or theme-based instruction that integrates other subject areas.

Describing the Writing Process

Making a quilt is a good metaphor for the process of writing. Many small squares with different patterns and colors contribute to the overall masterpiece. Although we may not know the process the quilter used, we believe there is a specific method. Similar to quilting, a writer uses small morsels or ideas with different patterns to craft a story. There is not one exclusive way to describe the composing process writers engage in. Some theorists describe this process as prewriting, writing, and rewriting; some call it circling out and circling back or collecting and connecting (Calkins, 1994). Researcher Donald Murray (1989) uses the terms rehearsal, drafting, revision, and editing, which are the terms used in writing workshops. These steps describe what occurs as writers continue through their development.

Regardless of what you are writing, a poem or a scientific research report, most writers often move through these same stages. Some writers spend more time on rehearsal, others on revision. Likewise, some writers may revise a work-related document many times and spend less time working on a personal letter. Certainly, the purpose of the written piece and the audience will often determine how you proceed through the process, but ultimately you will use the same process for each piece of writing. Although these steps are discussed separately, in reality there is a fine line between them, and they tend to blend together quite often.

Rehearsal

Rehearsal is the first step in the writing process before you actually sit down and begin to brainstorm ideas for a story. Rehearsal includes mental notes you make when you notice or admire something. It may be a photograph, a favorite toy or doll, or a memory.

> **The notebook is a place where students can jot down observations, questions, memories, and responses to books or stories they have read as they try to make sense of the world around them.**

A writer's notebook is a wonderful tool for rehearsal. If your students are too young to write in their own notebooks, a class notebook will serve the same purpose. The writer's notebook is similar to a scrapbook or family journal; it is a collection of ideas, jokes, stories, phrases, sentences, drawings, and significant objects. Each page can have a separate entry. The notebook is a place where students can jot down observations, questions, memories, and responses to books or stories they have read as they try to make sense of the world around them. Some researchers call this notebook a "journal," a "daybook," or a "container." No matter what term you choose to use, they are all places for rehearsal or, metaphorically speaking, a plot of fresh dirt where ideas are planted and stories will grow.

Rehearsal refers to a place where children are free to write their entries and later go back to choose one or two to create a story. Often when children are asked to write a story, they respond, "I can't think of anything." In these instances children can refer to the writer's notebook for ideas or questions that were interesting to them at one time; hopefully, the notebook will spark some interest and stimulate the energy needed to write. Ideas for journal or notebook entries can be generated from across the curriculum. **Some science and health topic ideas can be found in the activity on the next page.** Animals are a favorite topic for young children; therefore, many journal entries may be related to this topic.

Drafting

Drafting is simply putting words on paper and letting ideas flow without worrying about spelling, organization, and penmanship. Drafts are messy with words crossed out and arrows drawn in the margins. Drafts reflect the changes in your thoughts as you trudge through the writing process.

Science/Health

If you could be any animal in the world, what would you be and why?

If you could have any kind of animal for a pet, which would you choose?

What problems can pets cause, and how would you deal with them?

Create a riddle about your favorite animal.

Reprinted from TCM 505—Jump Into Journals

Revisions

Revising is an opportunity for students to read their drafts and revisit the entries in their notebooks (or the class notebook) to generate more ideas to add to their drafts. Often, many students revise as they draft, therefore, it is difficult to separate these two steps in the process of writing. In the writing workshop, revision is the essential element of conferences and mini-lessons.

When children conference with each other, they encourage the author to talk more about his or her topic and make a list of future entries the author might write as he or she lives with the topic and thinks about the topic. Each time an author revisits drafts with a different perspective, a new story is crafted.

> **Each time an author revisits drafts with a different perspective, a new story is crafted.**

Editing

Editing is part of the revision that includes specific attention to content, such as wording, elaboration of ideas, and details and mechanics, such as spelling and punctuation. It is during this stage students will turn to the dictionary and thesaurus for answers. Editing provides an opportunity for students to notice the conventions of written language around them. Mini-lessons on editing will often focus on a specific mechanics skill, such as the use of quotation marks in dialogue, capitalization, semicolons, and so forth.

Students need guidance and encouragement during the editing stage, which can be quite frustrating. It is essential that students learn the importance of editing as beginning writers. If the author feels his or her piece of writing is the best he or she can do and does not want to write anymore, then the writer can edit that piece. For young writers, the editing stage may only include a check for name, date, and title. As writers become more experienced, other skills can be added to the editing stage. A checklist is a helpful editing tool for children to use at the editing table in the classroom. Children need to know that editing is not only for correcting mechanical errors but also to make sure they did not leave out any details and their writing piece reads smoothly.

An editing conference between you and your students is helpful for you to show your students how to edit a piece. However, be sure to remember the author has the control over the piece. During an editing conference it is helpful for you to ask questions of the author, but do not overwhelm the writer with questions about content and mechanics all at once. Instead, focus on the primary problem the student seems to be having, and then you can help them the most rather than focusing on many little errors. Also, you can use an editing conference to try to understand the writer's logic since most errors grow out of some misunderstanding of conventions. When you understand the thought processes behind students' errors, you can guide, support, and help them in a way that will extend their own understanding.

Writing Materials

A variety of writing materials accessible to all children is a key component in a successful writing workshop classroom. Children enjoy experimenting with different writing utensils, such as pencils, pens, crayons, markers, and colored pencils, as well as different kinds of paper, lined, unlined, and colored. Journals and notebooks can also be found in writing workshop classrooms. The important thing is that students have the opportunity to decide which medium they want to use to express their own ideas. Computers are a new medium for students to use to write and publish their stories, which will be discussed in detail later in this chapter. **On the following page is a resource list of materials for a publishing center in your classroom.** All of these materials are not needed; use your judgement as to what is appropriate for your students. Remember that publishing a story is an exciting accomplishment; therefore, some extra attention should be paid to this component of the writing process.

Organization of children's writing is another key component in a successful writing workshop classroom. You will need folders or portfolios for filing drafts and works-in-progress. Make sure you have a filing system in place before you begin writing workshop because the management of drafts, revisions, notes, and finished pieces can be daunting. Storage of these files is important; remember that you will be accessing these files quite frequently, so do not store them high up on a closet shelf which is difficult to reach on a daily basis.

You will need to create a writing corner with tables and chairs and a bookcase with writing supplies, reference books, and other resources. Some teachers even recommend for peer or teacher conferencing a separate "Do Not Disturb" table where interruptions are not allowed. Tables and chairs throughout the classroom must be flexible and conducive to writing workshop activities. Walking space is important for children to move around the room to confer with peers, meet in infor-

> A variety of writing materials accessible to all children is a key component in a successful writing workshop classroom.

Publishing Center

Students need a place to be creative and to make their writing publishable. Some students will want to illustrate their work. Some will want to mount what they have done on colored paper. Others will want to add texture, magazine pictures, or cutout lettering. A publishing center provides students this opportunity. If possible, try to set up this center in an area where supplies do not have to be put away and taken out again. Here is a list of possible supplies for your publishing center.

SUPPLIES

pens in a variety of colors	crayons
regular and colored pencils	paint
pencil sharpener	watercolors
markers in a variety of point sizes	tagboard
calligraphy pens	stapler
construction paper	hole punch
lined and unlined paper	glue
old file folders	tape
wallpaper samples	scissors
contact paper	rulers
colored chalk	stencils
fixative	erasers
needles and thread	string
tissue paper	ribbon
old magazines and newspapers	stickers
greeting cards	old photographs
clipboard	sponges
stamp pads and a variety of stamps	straws
fabric scraps	pressed plants
paintbrushes in all sizes	wax paper
looseleaf rings	cellophane
scraps of yarn	food coloring
old shirts for smocks	worktable
typewriter or word processor	paper towels
bookbinder and plastic spines	cleaning cloths
laminating supplies or access	paper cutter
water for cleanup	parent volunteer

Reprinted from TCM 500—Write All About It: Grades 1–3

mal groups to discuss ideas or drafts, and have access to the materials or files. Additionally, the walking space is important for you to be able to move around the room freely to sit and listen to your students or to simply observe them up close. It is important your students understand that you are a member of the writing community, and if you sit down to listen to them, you are interested in what they have to say, not checking up on them.

Writing workshop classrooms also require the flexibility for furniture to be rearranged at the end of each session so the class can gather to hear selected children share works-in-progress or finished pieces. A permanent floor space set aside for informal class gatherings would be ideal if room permits. Otherwise, light furniture which is easily moved can work just as well for the "Author's Chair" where a child sits when he or she is sharing his or her work with the class. The "Author's Chair" should be special so the author feels special. A director's chair with colorful canvas is great, or a plastic lawn chair which is durable can also work well. The significant message is that when the author sits in the special chair to share a piece of writing, the other children show their respect.

The Structure of Writing Workshop

There are three major events which constitute the writing workshop:

- mini-lessons
- writing time and conferences
- sharing time.

A writing workshop classroom is a busy place since many activities take place during each of these events, and sometimes many activities occur simultaneously. A fundamental component in the philosophy of writing workshop is that you are creating a community of writers, and the individuals in this community interact, discuss, and share with one another in the process of writing texts. These interactions and discussions transpire before, during, and after the three events of mini-lessons, writing time and conferences, and sharing time.

Mini-Lessons

Mini-lessons are short instructional lessons in which something specific is being taught. Mini-lessons occur at the beginning of each writing workshop session, last only five to ten minutes, and end with a status report from each child.

> A fundamental component in the philosophy of writing workshop is that you are creating a community of writers, and the individuals in this community interact, discuss, and share with one another in the process of writing texts.

The status report allows children to identify their working goal for the day. Early in the year, the purpose of the mini-lessons is to introduce students to a writing workshop and focus on workshop procedures and protocols. Nancie Atwell (1987) uses her first mini-lesson to (1) model her own thinking process as she considers topics she would like to write about and the thinking and rehearsal she does before actually beginning to write, (2) guide students in selecting their first writing topic for the year, and (3) establish workshop guidelines (Ruddell and Ruddell, 1995, p. 334).

These three elements of Nancie Atwell's first mini-lesson engage children immediately into writing workshop behaviors and set the tone for how the workshop will be structured throughout the year. It is important that you set up a similar structure for your students so they know what to expect and also learn about your thinking and prewriting processes. Share some of your writing experiences with your students so they feel that you are part of the community of writers. Also, share some of your writing pieces with them, preferably a piece that has been through revisions and was very important to you, such as a letter to a friend, a poem to a loved one, or a letter to an editor voicing your opinion or concern about an issue.

> **Share some of your writing experiences with your students so they feel that you are part of the community of writers.**

In the beginning of the year, your mini-lessons may be setting up rituals rather than doing writing activities. Some teachers develop the ritual of "Notebook News," which is a time when students can share with the class anything from their notebooks: ideas, phrases, sentences, poems, or pictures. Or students can share something new in their notebooks, a joke or a drawing, which is a way for students to share how their notebooks have become a part of their daily lives. This is a ritual that will highlight the importance of the notebook as a tool for rehearsal. Any entry a student wants to talk about is fine, and some students may even add onto an entry once they have shared it with the class and received some feedback.

Another ritual other teachers develop early in the year is a ceremony in which students open their notebooks to a particular page and leave it on their desks as part of a "Notebook Museum" (Calkins, 1994). As writers walk around the room, glancing at their classmates' notebooks, they notice different ways students write their ideas and observations. This ritual celebrates the diversity of the notebooks and the diversity of the writers. After the students have walked around, they discuss things they noticed and new ideas they might try based on what they saw in the "Notebook Museum."

The Notebook News and Notebook Museum rituals are just a few ideas of how to engage students in the process of writing and sustain their interest. Think of ways you can make rituals a significant part of your writing workshop classroom and try to keep the ideas flowing. It is not easy to keep writing alive over a long period of time; however, with variations of ideas, these rituals can also work in a math or social studies or science curriculum, which will contribute to the writer's imagination.

Later in the year mini-lessons may consist of using a piece of children's writing to teach about capitalization or punctuation. **On the following page is a group of activities on capitalization and punctuation you can use in your mini-lessons.** The task cards provided are to be used to develop the skills of capitalization and punctuation. It is helpful to teach these skills using students' writing, making it more meaningful to them. Take the initiative and design some of your own task cards on other grammatical skills that you can use in your mini-lessons.

Other topics for mini-lessons may include visiting another classroom and telling your students what you observed or giving ideas of how your students can broaden their range of writing from stories or letters to plays and poetry. Integrating literature into your mini-lessons is a wonderful way of generating good writing. Discussions of writing styles used by particular authors, such as Bill Martin, Jr., Dr. Seuss, or Richard Scary can be helpful mini-lessons for your students as well as an opportunity to deepen their understanding of good writing. During these mini-lessons discuss the qualities of good writing you want your students to strive for (lots of details, excitement, and concrete information) and invite them to share their visions of good writing.

Some writing guidelines that Nancie Atwell (1987) suggests will encourage your students to become members of the writing community in your classroom:

Do not erase; instead, draw a line through it so you can record your thinking and any changes.

Write on one side of the paper only. It is easier to manually cut and paste when writing is only on one side.

Save everything; you may want to go back to earlier ideas.

Date and label everything. Mark your papers with appropriate labels, such as "Draft #1" or "Notes."

Speak in quiet voices only. Most children need quiet time to think and write, but make sure you designate an area in the classroom where children can each work with a friend and discuss their writing.

Work really hard. Time is never wasted when writing.

> It is not easy to keep writing alive over a long period of time; however, with variations of ideas, these rituals can also work in a math or social studies or science curriculum, which will contribute to the writer's imagination.

Writing Skills Task Cards

TASK CARD: *Capitalization*

In the classroom on the wall under the clock, your teacher has posted a story with nine capitalization errors. Find them!

Rewrite the story with the corrections you have found.

TASK CARD: *Capitalization*

In the writing center you will find a cereal box. Rewrite a short part of something that is written on it, only as you write, make five capitalization errors.

Give your paper with errors to a friend to edit.

TASK CARD: *Capitalization*

Write a few sentences using the names of five people and places, but do not write these names with capitals.

Give your paper to a partner. See if he or she can be a successful capitalization detective!

TASK CARD: *Punctuation*

Read one or more of the pages from a book at this table. Recopy several of the sentences without end punctuation.

Give your paper with errors to a friend to edit.

TASK CARD: *Punctuation*

Read the paper posted on the wall by the door. Each time you see a comma, pause. Each time you see an end punctuation mark, take a breath.

Use this technique as you write your own papers or as you edit the papers of others.

TASK CARD: *Punctuation*

Make a list of contractions without putting apostrophes where they belong.

Give your paper to a partner. See if he or she can be a successful punctuation detective!

Reprinted from TCM 500—Write All About It: Grades 1–3

These guidelines can be helpful to you when creating our own writing workshop rules and regulations. However, keep in mind that "procedural structure is important to the success of the entire writing workshop venture" (Ruddell and Ruddell, 1995, p. 336).

Writing Time and Conferences

The majority of your writing workshop time is devoted to writing time and conferences. Preferably, at least thirty minutes per day should be devoted to these activities and perhaps longer, depending on your students. A good way to transition from mini-lessons into writing time is what Nancie Atwell (1987) calls "status-of-the-class-roll-call report." Basically you should take three to four minutes to poll your students about their progress by asking them, "What are you doing today?" This will give them a chance to focus on exactly what they need to do on their writing piece. Atwell (1987) recommends teaching your students "writer's language" such as "draft, revise, abandon, conference, and edit" so they can quickly answer the question of what they are working on that particular day. It is a good idea to keep track of each student's response in a teacher's journal or log book in the form of a table with appropriate abbreviations. For example, "D1" for first draft, "D2" for second draft, "AB" for abandon, "SE" for self-editing, "PE" for peer editing, "SC" for self-conference, "PC" for peer conference and "TC" for teacher conference. See the sample below of a teacher's log for the status-of-the-class poll.

> The majority of your writing workshop time is devoted to writing time and conferences.

Name	Mon.	Tue.	Wed.	Thurs.	Fri.
Caroline	D1	D1	SE	PE	TC
Brigid	D2	PE	PC	TC	SE
Jake	PE	PC	SE	SC	TC

Although it is very important for children to focus on writing, this roll call should be quick and informal. Remember, writing time is devoted to writing! For younger children in kindergarten and first grade, encourage them to draw pictures and write stories about the pictures to the best of their abilities. In a primary grade workshop, it is very likely that some children will be drawing, painting, writing, and scribbling while other students attempt to use conventional written forms. The children in your class will be at varying levels of writing, so it is essential that there are plenty of opportunities for them to experiment with writing, drawing, and scribbling.

For children learning English as a second language, they may use writing time as a time to sort out their understanding of their new language and create combinations of first language and English text, or they may use lots of pictures to support or replace written text. Some

ESL children and other students with language or learning differences may not want to write or draw; therefore, be sensitive to the needs of all the students in your class. Drawings and illustrations may be sufficient for them to work on during writing time.

During writing time, you will act as a guide to oversee the children's growth and development as writers. You will also act as their biggest fan and supporter. Encouragement can go a long way, especially for beginning writers. One way for you to express your support and encouragement is during conferences.

Throughout writing workshop, writers engage in many different kinds of conferences with teachers and with peers.

Throughout writing workshop, writers engage in many different kinds of conferences with teachers and with peers. It is during these conferences ideas are shared, responses are given, and children learn mechanics in context, as stated earlier in the seven principles that guide writing workshop. In the early stages of writing workshop, conferences are short and to the point and usually occur as the teacher floats around the room to check in with students as they engage in writing. Nancie Atwell (1987) offers the following guidelines for these types of conferences.

1. Keep it short—one to two minutes.
2. See as many writers each day as possible.
3. Go to your students, rather than having them come to you, so you can control the length of the conference.
4. Make eye contact with the writer by kneeling or sitting alongside his or her desk.
5. Do not tell writers what should be in their writing or, worse, write on their pieces.
6. Build on what writers know and have done.
7. Resist making judgments (positive or negative) about the writing and avoid contrived praise.
8. Ask about things that really interest you in the children's writing (Atwell, 1987, pp. 94 and 95).

Other types of conferences occur between teacher and child as the teacher floats around the room and spends about five minutes with a few children. Lucy Calkins calls these "longer, slower conferences" (1991) which should happen in response to children's needs. She emphasizes that "We are teaching the writer, not the writing" (1986, p. 120) in all conferences. Sharing authority with your students is an essential element in successful conferencing. Rather than imposing your ideas on your students, allow them to share their ideas with you and tell you how they are doing with their written text.

In addition to teacher conferences, writers engage in peer conferences during writing time. During peer conferences children work in partners or small groups, share their writing, and receive assistance and ideas for moving their writing forward. Peer editing will take place throughout peer conferences, especially for older children. Young children need to be taught how to peer conference and how to provide helpful feedback. You need to model how to conference with one another and plan on many mini-lessons that address this aspect of writing workshop. **On the following page is an activity that will teach students how to conduct a peer conference.** You should be able to adapt this activity to the level of your students. Peer conferences can be a very valuable part of writing workshop if they are executed successfully. Role-playing is a good way to show children how to participate in a peer conference. You might offer some easy guidelines for your students to follow, for example:

1. When listening to someone else's writing, try to find at least one thing you found interesting about the piece and tell the author.

2. Ask questions that will help the writers solve problems and improve their writing. Questions should begin "How could you...?" "How might you add more details?" "What do you want to say?" and so forth (Ruddell and Ruddell, 1994).

For older children, the mechanics of editing must be taught, which is a great way for you to sneak in a few grammar lessons in the context of students' written texts. Suggestions about sentences, paragraphs, and punctuation can be discussed in mini-lessons. **On page 55 is a list of editing symbols that you can introduce to your students one at a time during mini-lessons.** Only introduce these symbols if your students demonstrate an understanding of the use of each symbol. Explain that professional editors also use these symbols, so once they learn these symbols, they can use them throughout their writing careers.

Another form of conferences children engage in during writing workshop is the self-conference. This is when children silently read through their written pieces and metacognitively think about what questions other children might ask. "Pretend" reading and questioning is what younger children may call self-conferences. Lucy Calkins (1986, p. 19) suggests the following questions for structuring self-conferences:

- What have I said so far? What am I trying to say here?
- How do I like it? What's good here that I can build on? What's not so good that I can fix?
- How does it sound? How does it look?

> During peer conferences children work in partners or small groups, share their writing, and receive assistance and ideas for moving their writing forward.

The Peer Conference

Activity:

Students will learn to conduct a peer conference.

Materials:

- previously modeled story
- marking pen

Preparation:

Complete the activities

Directions:

A peer conference is the first opportunity for an author to receive feedback about his or her story. Both children have a job to do during a peer conference. The author is the reader who brings his or her writing notebook to the conference. The peer is the listener who brings ideas to the conference.

When the children have completed drafts of their stories, they are ready for peer conferences. Establish the following guidelines for a peer conference:

1. The author and peer sit close together with their knees touching. (This helps keep the noise level to a minimum and helps to keep them engaged in their jobs.)
2. The author brings his or her writing notebook and reads the story. The peer is the listener and thinker. He or she listens carefully to the story and then gives one or two ideas as to how the author can make the story better.
3. Peer listeners must give ideas for revising (making the story better).
4. After reading the story, the author and peer discuss ideas that will improve the story.
5. The author thanks the peer and returns to his or her writing to revise the story.

Give the children several examples of ideas a peer listener might give an author. For example:

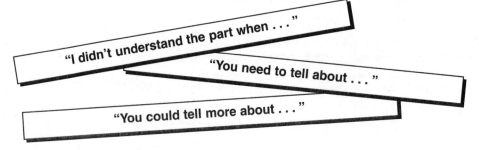

"I didn't understand the part when . . ."

"You need to tell about . . ."

"You could tell more about . . ."

Before the students conduct a peer conference on their own, model one for them, using the story you wrote previously or another you have written. It is helpful to have a peer (another teacher) do the modeling with you, if possible.

Reprinted from TCM 500—Write All About It: Grades 1–3

Proofreading Marks

Editor's Mark	Meaning	Example
≡	Capitalize	<u>d</u>avid gobbled up the grapes.
/	Make lowercase	My mother hugged Me when I came Home.
⊙	Add a period	The clouds danced in the sky⊙
Sp.	Spelling mistake	sp. I laffed at the story.
∽	Reverse words or letters	How you are?
∧	Add a word	please Would you ∧ pass the pizza?
⌄	Add a comma	I have two cats, two dogs∧and a goldfish.
ℓ	Delete (Get rid of)	Will you call call me on the phone tonight?

Reprinted from TCM 500—Write All About It: Grades 1–3

- How else could I have done this?
- What will my readers think as they read this?
- What questions will they ask? What will they notice? feel? think?
- What am I going to do next?

A few mini-lessons may address the list of questions and the process of self-conferences. You might want to keep a list of these questions in your writing center for children to refer to. For younger children, you may use a pictograph with happy faces and question marks for children to refer to when they listen to their peers.

Sharing Time

Sharing is an essential element in the writing workshop classroom, although it is not a "formal" component. Writers are encouraged to share throughout the writing process, from talking with a friend about an entry to reading the final draft of a story to the class in the "Author's Chair." During peer conferences, students share ideas, opinions, and interpretations of words, phrases, and pictures. And when a child sits in the "Author's Chair," the author should inform the audience as to what he or she is sharing. If it is a work-in-progress, suggestions and ideas about revisions may be solicited. On the other hand, if it is a finished piece, audience members may respond to interesting ideas and uses of details rather than giving suggestions for improvement.

The objective of sharing time is for students to understand the importance of an audience and to encourage the desire to share their stories. Children naturally want to share their stories with their friends, so by making it a formalized event and sitting in the "Author's Chair," reading their stories becomes a special part of the writing workshop. Lucy Calkins (1994) believes that we all have stories to tell and others want to hear our stories, which is why sharing time is an essential component in writers workshop.

The interactions that evolve from sharing stories will create the fabric of your classroom. Remember that writing can transform your classroom every day when children share a part of their lives. With each story, your community of learners deepens and changes forever (Calkins, 1994). Since writing allows children to have a voice, your classroom will become a forum for children to voice their beliefs, opinions, and interpretations of life. Children write about things that are real to them, and when they share their stories, the listeners will confirm their beliefs and fears through laughter and tears.

Remember that writing can transform your classroom every day when children share a part of their lives.

Publishing

Publishing is a formalized way of sharing a written piece. After writers have revised and edited their stories or poems, they are ready for the final drafts. Whether the final draft is presented as a few pages stapled together or in a clothbound book, the idea that the writer has reached the end of the process is an amazing accomplishment. When a writer completes the final draft and publishes it for everyone to read, he or she is proclaiming that he or she is a writer. Other forms of publishing include performance of a written piece, reading it aloud to an audience, or circulating it among readers. Some youngsters also like to "direct" the performance of their own story rather than star in it.

For many children, sharing and publishing are significant steps in their own literacy journey. They realize at an early age that sharing stories and illustrations brings satisfaction and happiness. Young children are extremely eager to read a story over and over and share their favorite parts. Similarly, young authors are eager to share their own personal stories with others as a way of allowing others to enter into their world.

> **For many children, sharing and publishing are significant steps in their own literacy journey.**

In light of the importance of sharing and publishing, it is imperative that you have an area in your classroom for displaying finished pieces of writing. A bulletin board or a designated wall works best. Also, a "Class Book," a collection of children's pieces of writing, is a popular class treasure that each child can contribute to after sitting in the "Author's Chair" and sharing a published story with the class. **Additional ideas for publishing are included on the following page.** You can adapt these ideas to the level of your students. Remember, publishing is a way of expressing ideas and celebrating the miracle of literacy. Each form of publishing is a well-deserved stride in the literacy journey of your students.

Electronic Forms of Publishing

Publishing takes on a whole new meaning with the integration of technology into our classrooms. Children's stories can be published on the computer, printed with colored ink, and have a professional-style cover. Importing graphics and pictures or creating original illustrations in a paint or draw software program is an easy way to illustrate stories, especially for self-conscious artists. Another form of publishing can include a class or school Web page, which is a place on the Web where students can "post" their writing and receive feedback from other children around the world. Numerous writing contests are held on the Internet and various Web pages, which motivates children to write for a larger audience.

Publishing Ideas

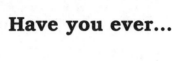

Have you ever...

Worn it on a T-shirt? asked to tack it to a community
bulletin board?...phoned it to a grandparent?...
served it on a platter?...sung it with a guitar?...
framed it? ...read it aloud?...had it published in a
parents' newsletter?...written it in watercolor?...
taped it as a radio program?...sent it to a local
newspaper?...bound it in a book?...hung it in your
room?...performed it for an assembly?...written it in
fresh snow?...read it in a poetry parade?...sent it
to a nursing home?...read it over the school's public
address system?...written it in a cookbook?...
drawn it on a graffiti mural with permission?...sent it
to a sick classmate?...written it to a pen pal?...told
it to a pet?...presented it in an animated film or
comic strip?...written it in chalk on your driveway?...
made a poster of it?...entered it in a contest?...
flown it across the room on a paper airplane?...
stitched it on fabric?...written it on an original
calendar you have tried to sell?...performed it in a
puppet show?...bound it and placed it in the library?
...sent it in a letter to a published author?...made it
a message in a bottle?...written it in sand?...sent it
to a political figure such as your mayor, senator,
representative, or the president?...performed it as a
skit in a shopping mall?...submitted it to a magazine?
...read it to a school employee such as the principal's
secretary or a cafeteria worker?...Magic-Marked it on
a sheet?...mailed it to a former teacher?...saved it in
a time capsule for the future?...sent it in a class
mailbox?... illustrated it for a Valentine?...read it to the
class?...tucked it away to be read and enjoyed when
you are older?

Reprinted from TCM 500—Write All About It: Grades 1–3

A variety of word processing and paint and draw software programs provide opportunities for children to publish their writing in a new medium. *KidPix* is a favorite authoring program for young children, which offers pictures, stamps, and ideas for children to use in their stories. *Stanley's Sticker Stories* is another popular software program that offers different story settings, such as the playground or the classroom. The authors can place stickers where they want to and then write stories to accompany the scenes they have created. Software programs such as those mentioned above encourage children to create new settings and characters and add new vocabulary words to their "word boxes."

The technology is only enhancing what the child wants to do, which is to write and share his or her stories. Keep in mind publishing on the computer is just as wonderful as a handmade book and should be treated as equally important.

Concluding Remarks

The Nobel laureate author Toni Morrison considers her written pieces to be in "constant revision" even after they have been published. She explains that she can always find places for new ideas when she revisits her published books or as she reads the *New York Times* each day. As you work with your children during the process of writing, you must remind them that even our expert writers go through the same process. As writers, we may never want to let go of our writing pieces, but at some point we must. Toni Morrison's term, "constant revision," is a mantra for all writers.

A variety of word processing and paint and draw software programs provide opportunities for children to publish their writing in a new medium.

Reading and Writing Activities for Older Children

Project-Based Writing

Therefore, inquiry is the starting point and sustaining element of a classroom project and the driving force behind project-based writing.

Project-based writing centers around a major project a class chooses to undertake, hence the title. It may be a yearlong project, such as a class yearbook, or a short-term project, such as monthly class newsletters. Jerry Harste (1994), a prominent researcher of young children, places emphasis on the importance of inquiry as the foundation for project-based writing. He defines "inquiry" as a deep desire to know rather than a methodology of research. He states, "Viewing curriculum as inquiry means that I envision classrooms as sites of inquiry, or as communities of learners. Inquiry is not a technical skill to be applied at will, but rather a philosophical stance that permeates the kinds of lives we choose to live" (1994, pp. 1,230–1,231). Therefore, inquiry is the starting point and sustaining element of a classroom project and the driving force behind project-based writing.

An easy way to describe project-based writing is through the use of the "authoring cycle" which is quite similar to the writing process and the procedures discussed earlier in the writing workshop. Harste and Short (1988) use the authoring cycle to capture the essence of the daily writing in the classroom. The authoring cycle begins with life experiences, uninterrupted reading and writing, author's folder, author's circle, self-editing, outside editor, publishing/celebrating authorship, invitations/language strategy instruction, and so on. Similar to writing workshop, the authoring cycle encourages children to use life experiences and knowledge to create stories. It is much easier to write about something we are familiar with and about things we want to know more about. Therefore, the notion of inquiry, as Harste envisions, is a powerful element in our thinking about writing. He encourages teachers and children to examine what they know, take a look around their world, and decide what it is they want to know more about. "Then all writing and learning should grow from class exploration of questions generated in determining what the group wants to know" (Ruddell and Ruddell, 1994, p. 350).

> Based on the notion of inquiry, the curriculum should be guided by choices of teachers and children rather than state and district mandates.

Based on the notion of inquiry, the curriculum should be guided by choices of teachers and children rather than state and district mandates. Also, writing assignments stemming from the inquiry topic may be more authentic. Inquiry, then, is the basis of project-based writing. Consider, for a moment, how much more exciting it would be to write about a field trip to the zoo, including descriptions of the animals, diets, and habitats, rather than simply showing pictures to your students and asking them to answer questions about what an animal eats. A field trip project can generate many ideas and forms of writing, such as poems, books, and newspaper articles. Children will most likely enjoy writing from their own experiences.

Integrating project-based writing into your class is not difficult, according to Harste (1994). Simply begin by leading a discussion with your students about "Things We Know" (Harste, 1994). Encourage children to work in pairs or small groups and then create a class list together. On the next day, have your students generate a list of "Things We Do Not Know" and then on the following day, "Things We Want to Know." With youngsters, these lists can be generated as a whole class activity. This discussion may last a few days to a week, but it is important that children have time to think about their ideas. Once you have a list, you can begin to decide with the class on a project that will be interesting to most of your students (it may be difficult to please all of your students) and think about writing activities that are appropriate for the project. Offer multiple possibilities for publishing a project-related book, newsletter, or magazine. It is imperative that you also develop procedures and record-keeping systems before you begin the project so you are not overwhelmed. You may want to incorporate into your plan the status-of-the-class roll call each day and the three-minute logging of daily accomplishments, as discussed in writing workshop in the previous chapter.

Theme Cycles

Theme cycles are similar to inquiry projects yet very different. They are more appropriate for older children but can be modified with kindergarten and first graders. Bess Altwerger and Barbara Flores (1991) describe theme cycles as cycles of study in which children negotiate the theme for instruction through class discussions and question/answer sessions. In theme cycles, children do most of the planning and carrying out of activities and writing, similar to project-based writing. The teacher does not predetermine the topic and materials; these are determined by the class discussions. Sharing authority is an essential element in the successful execution of theme cycles. The teacher should guide in planning writing opportunities to accompany the theme cycle and encourage writers to develop ideas and clarify their thinking through writing. Then, finally, students share and publish their writing with the class and, perhaps, a larger audience.

> The primary goal of both project-based writing and theme cycles is to engage students in their own learning by finding out what it is that they want to learn.

The primary goal of both project-based writing and theme cycles is to engage students in their own learning by finding out what it is that they want to learn. Then it is up to the teacher to integrate their desires and wants with the curriculum and content areas and provide appropriate literacy events. You may want to start off on a small scale and build onto your project or theme each year, based on your success.

Pen Pal Projects

The pen pal project is a popular writing activity in classrooms of older children. It is an activity in which the children write to a pen pal, wait for a response, and may continue to write back and forth for a long period of time, depending on the ages of the students. With younger children, writing one letter may be sufficient.

The pen pals can be in the same class, the same school, or completely in another class far away. This project can begin as a class project by sending a class letter to another class and waiting for a response, or you may organize the correspondence with another class of students and assign pen pals to your students. Another enjoyable way of initiating the pen pal project is to have students choose names out of a hat. Regardless of how pen pals are chosen, it is more important for children to enjoy the process of writing a letter to a new friend and understand the value of written correspondence.

The pen pal project can easily be integrated into other curricular areas, especially a social studies unit on geography and communities. Pen pal projects can also be integrated into art, music, and language arts units. The story *The Jolly Postman* by Janet and Allan Ahlberg is a wonderful piece of literature that can be read to the children to begin a discussion of written correspondence. A discussion of the different kinds of letters to write and how letters are delivered to their pen pals may transpire.

Depending on the location of your pen pals, children can brainstorm questions to ask their pen pals to learn more about them. In addition to the basic questions, "What is your name?" and "Where do you live?" some suggested questions your students might ask their pen pals are the following:

- What is your favorite food?
- What kinds of books do you like to read?
- What kinds of games do you like to play?
- What is the weather like today?

> Regardless of how pen pals are chosen, it is more important for children to enjoy the process of writing a letter to a new friend and understand the value of written correspondence.

Through participation in a pen pal project, children can learn the importance of expressing their ideas in the form of a letter. They can also experience writing to an unknown audience, which is a significant step in the process of writing. **Learning the correct format of a letter can be accomplished using the activity on the following page.** Understanding the parts of the letter can be difficult for young children; however, if there is a poster hanging in the writing center, they can refer to this poster when writing any kind of a letter.

Electronic key pals is a popular activity with the integration of technology into many classrooms. This is a great project for children to learn how to type and how to write. For younger children the teacher can type an e-mail message generated from class discussions. Older children can type the message themselves, perhaps, after some rehearsal and drafting. An e-mail message is another form of publishing a written piece. Sometimes older children will share poems or stories with their key pals.

Parts-of-a-Letter Poster

If desired, let the students color the poster and then laminate it for durability. Display it during all your letter writing activities.

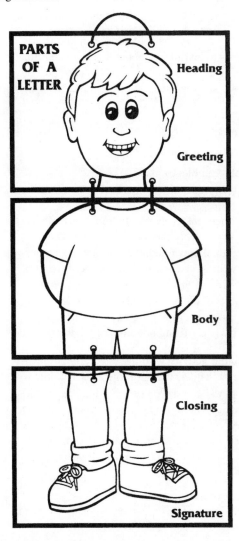

Reprinted from TCM 500—Write All About It: Grades 1–3

Reading Activities in the Classroom

The classroom community is a setting where children learn to read through interactions and dialogues with both peers and teachers through horizontal and vertical scaffolding, respectively. This section will focus on the reading activities that involve teacher/student interactions as well as peer interactions. Regardless of age or grade level, a community of learners will have similar influences on a child, especially while the child is learning to read and acquiring oral and written language.

Many years ago, Dewey (1916) encouraged schools to exist as a community of learners where children can grow and mature. Indeed, the classroom is a place where children are free to grow and develop their thoughts through interactions and experiences with others. It is then that children discover their individuality within a community of learners involving participation and reflection. Through specific activities that transpire in the classroom, children learn to read and write with the help of others. Various literacy activities include building vertically and horizontally on others' responses while connecting and referring to other texts in other dialogues. The specific activities that will be discussed are reading aloud (story sharing), cross-aged reading buddies, and partner reading.

Reading Aloud or Story Sharing

Reading aloud is a traditional classroom practice appropriate for all grades (Ruddell & Ruddell, 1995), not only emergent learners. In many ways, the teacher is modeling fluency in oral language and enjoyment in literature and scaffolding the children while providing opportunity for reader response and active comprehension. This activity can be implemented with a small group of students or the whole class across all grade levels and abilities. Additionally, it can be an extended activity, for example, reading a chapter in a book or reading a different story each day. Either way, the reading aloud experience is a chance to share stories in the classroom.

During the shared story time, the teacher asks questions that encourage the children to problem solve and search for answers that they may not figure out on their own. The children, then, interconnect previous experiences and weave in others' ideas and thoughts when responding. Additionally, the discussion that evolves through story sharing encourages children to adopt a social voice which then contributes to the understanding of the story. Creating links to other texts and transforming inner speech to oral language is a result of reading-aloud activities.

> The classroom community is a setting where children learn to read through interactions and dialogues with both peers and teachers through horizontal and vertical scaffolding, respectively.

When the teacher shares a story and discusses it, the child internalizes the social actions and later shares the same story or a new story with a peer. When children share a story, they often combine their own thoughts with the thoughts of others. With guidance from the teacher, the child is encouraged to participate in a culturally valued activity. Sharing stories is an activity that is valued in most cultures, especially the school culture. Reading-aloud activities involving teachers and students that occur within the zone of proximal development can bridge the gap between a child's actual and potential developmental levels through problem solving. It is through these assisted interactions that a child learns to read and sustains the motivation to read.

Cross-Aged Reading Buddies

A more specific reading-aloud activity, cross-aged reading buddies, involves two students, an older one and a younger one, who work together, taking turns to read with each other on a daily basis. If the younger child does not know how to read, then the older reading buddy will read most of the story and encourage the younger one to guess what will happen in the story. During the activity, both participants discuss the story and engage in an extension activity which could be reading a similar story, writing about the story, acting out a favorite part of the story, or drawing a picture.

The activity benefits both participants; the older student improves his or her oral language fluency while the younger student becomes more involved in the reading process.

Throughout this activity, meanings and ideas are negotiated between readers, and new meanings are constructed through the conversations about the story. The younger student is guided through the activity while participating in it.

The extension activity can involve both verbal and nonverbal interactions. The students may have a dialogue about the story, or they may choose to draw pictures expressing their feelings the story evoked. The latter choice is an example of nonverbal social interaction, which is as equally important as verbal social interactions. Both kinds of interactions are different tools from the tool kit, as Wertsch (1991) explains, that individuals select to accomplish the task. This activity, then, allows students to take diverse approaches when interacting with others and learning to read.

Partner Reading

Partner reading involves two children who take turns reading together and talking about the story. This is a form of peer collaboration when two or more students work together to produce something that neither could have produced alone.

> The activity benefits both participants; the older student improves his or her oral language fluency while the younger student becomes more involved in the reading process.

When engaged in conversations, children weave into the conversations past experiences in response to others' ideas and thoughts. It is through the conversations that each partner adopts a social voice, and through the social interaction, multiple voices are developed. Therefore, the conversation encourages children to interconnect prior knowledge and experiences that assist in the comprehension of the story.

Sometimes during partner reading with older children, the partners help each other solve problems, figure out the meanings of different words, and decode unfamiliar words. Usually, the partners take turns predicting what will happen next in the story and turn it into a guessing game.

Partner reading and other peer collaborated activities are important social interactions that influence learning to read and encourage the learner to grow and develop literacy skills with the help of a peer. The interaction that occurs during partner reading and other peer collaborated activities is most common in the school setting but is also found in the home environment during playtime with friends.

There are many extensions to partner reading, including partner book sharing (Ruddell & Ruddell, 1995), which may involve sharing their interests and responses and peer conferencing, which is a vital component of the writing workshop and requires partners to read and evaluate each other's papers.

Connecting experiences, thoughts, and responses with teachers and peers through various reading and writing activities allows one to grow and develop as an individual and continue on his or her literacy journey.

Concluding Remarks

In sum, these reading and writing activities are prevalent in the classroom community and encourage children to grow and become mature readers and writers through observation, participation, and reflection. These activities involve social interaction and language learning and contribute to the development of a community of learners within the classroom. Connecting experiences, thoughts, and responses with teachers and peers through various reading and writing activities allows one to grow and develop as an individual and continue on his or her literacy journey.

Assessment Principles

It is vital to remember that assessment is not random but that there are principles that guide the process of evaluation and assessment.

Authentic Assessment Principles

Our beliefs and understandings about assessment have dramatically changed over the past two decades. The 1970s and early 1980s viewed assessment as a behavioral objective that could be measured solely by standardized tests. Assessment was synonymous with the term accountability. Fortunately, we now understand that assessment should be situated in authentic classroom learning, which means we should observe children as they engage in literacy events in the classroom.

It is vital to remember that assessment is not random but that there are principles that guide the process of evaluation and assessment. Ruddell and Ruddell (1995) offer seven principles of assessment that derive from an authentic assessment perspective.

1. Assessment should be primarily based on observations of children engaged in authentic classroom reading and writing tasks.

2. Assessment should focus on children's learning and the instructional goals of your curriculum.

3. Assessment should be continuous, based on observations over a substantial period of time.

4. Assessment should take into account the diversity of students' cultural, language, and special needs.

5. Assessment should be collaborative and include the active participation of children.

6. Assessment should recognize the importance of using a variety of observations rather than relying on one assessment approach.

7. Assessment must be knowledge-based and reflect our most current understanding of reading and writing processes.

Assessment allows us to be truly student centered in our teaching (Calkins, 1994). Rather than teaching directly to a standardized test or to the state framework, authentic assessment allows teachers to focus on their students. Teachers are encouraged to search within their classes for evidence that their students are learning. Growth and progress should not be determined by scores on a test; instead, students should be given the opportunity to show what they have learned over time through an assessment tool, such as a portfolio. However, with the rise in popularity of portfolios as a method of evaluating children's writing progress, there are common misconceptions and misuses that can lead to "unauthentic assessment." Calkins (1994) cautions that a portfolio is a record of a writer's journey, not a collection of best work. It should include drafts, edited versions, and final pieces, as well as works-in-progress and the low points and breakthroughs of a writer's career.

Abandoning standardized tests and looking within your classroom does not imply that assessment should be random; on the contrary, assessment needs to be aligned with instruction. Calkins (1994) proclaims that if we are to implement inquiry methods of learning science, cooperative learning, hands-on math, thematic units, and reading and writing workshops, there need to be appropriate assessment methods in place to assess students' growth and progress. Appropriate is the operative word. Certainly, there is not only one assessment instrument that has the capability to assess students' growth and progress in all subject areas.

The purposes of assessment instruments are to learn more about your students in order to design your teaching to respond to their needs and to assess their progress in your class. Teachers need to be reminded to make meaning from what they learn about their students and, ultimately, how that knowledge can guide instruction. Specific assessment instruments grow out of values in your class. If exploration, discovery, and inquiry are values you espouse in your teaching, you should use the assessment instruments that will appreciate and best reflect those particular values. Classroom observations, running records, interest inventories, and portfolios are the most likely assessment instruments you might want to use.

Concluding Remarks

Assessment is a critical component of the writing and reading processes. It is also a critical factor in guiding instructional strategies. Whatever assessment instruments you choose to use in your classroom, be sure that they will improve your teaching and your students' learning. Collecting artifacts for a writer's portfolio is relatively simple; the difficult part is to decide what to do with the information you collect. Therein lie the true benefits of authentic forms of assessment.

Growth and progress should not be determined by scores on a test; instead, students should be given the opportunity to show what they have learned over time through an assessment tool, such as a portfolio.

69

The Journey Continues

Reading and writing are intricately related to every learning activity children engage in.

Reflections on the Literacy Journey

In the first chapter you were asked to think about the importance of reading and writing in your life. Recall your reflections on the process you went through to become a fluent reader and writer. These memories of reading stories with your parents or writing letters to a grandparent are all important experiences in your lifelong literacy journey. Now think about the literacy journey your students embark upon each day in your classroom. In the previous chapters you were provided with opportunities to build your own understanding of the literacy journey. Each chapter offered theories, ideas, activities, and insights into the reading and writing processes your students engage in each time they read, write, speak, or listen.

In this book I have provided you with a framework to use when conceptualizing the challenges of literacy in your classroom. Reading and writing are intricately related to every learning activity children engage in. The process of writing has evolved into a way of life for teachers and children. Rather than assigning meaningless writing drills, teachers should encourage children to write about what is important to them. Integrating personal knowledge and experiences into the classroom is a good start as is allowing children to choose the topics to write about, such as in project-based writing or theme cycles. Becoming a young author is a turning point for many children, and it is with encouragement and guidance that your students can become proud authors.

Implementing a strong writing program in your classroom is an essential element in your curriculum planning. It is hoped that the ideas in this book will contribute to new thoughts on planning reading and writing lessons for your students. Learning more about the constructivist perspective driving the latest reform movement or gaining information on assessment principles will strengthen the writing program in your classroom.

Living the writer's life requires students to weave writing into the fabric of their lives in your classroom, at home, or on the playground. By empowering your students with the gift of writing, new perspectives on learning and life will emerge. When literacy is celebrated with family and friends, students will eagerly continue on their lifelong literacy journey. The only way to know if they continue on their journey is to wait for a letter from one of your students, thanking you for your words of wisdom and the support and encouragement. Then you will know that they are on their ways to wonderful literate lives.

By empowering your students with the gift of writing, new perspectives on learning and life will emerge.

References

Ahlberg, J., & Ahlberg, A. (1986). The jolly postman. New York: Little Brown.

Altwerger, B., & Flores, B. (1991). Theme cycles: An overview. In K. S. Goodman, L. B. Bird, & Y. M. Goodman (Eds.). The whole language catalog. New York: Macmillan.

Atwell, N. (1987). In the middle. Portsmouth, NH: Heinemann.

Bloome, D. (1985). Bedtime story reading as a social process. National Reading Conference Yearbook, 34, 287-294.

Bloome, D. (Ed.). (1986). Literacy and schooling. Norwood, NJ: Ablex.

Briggs, J. B. (1991, June 9). Writers do it daily. This World, p. 4.

Bruner, J. (1978). The role of dialogue in language acquisition. In A. Sinclair, R. J. Jarvelle, & W.J.M. Leveet (Eds.). The child's conception of language. New York: Springer.

Bruner, J. (1986). Actual minds, possible worlds. Cambridge, MA: Harvard University Press.

Butler, A., & Turnbill, J. (1984). Towards a reading-writing classroom. Rozelle, NSW: Primary English Teaching Association.

Calkins, L. M. (1986). The art of teaching writing. (1st ed.) Portsmouth, NH: Heinemann.

Calkins, L. M. (1991). Living between the lines. Portsmouth, NH: Heinemann.

Calkins, L. M. (1994). The art of teaching writing. (2nd ed.) Portsmouth, NH: Heinemann.

Clay, M. M. (1966). Emergent reading behavior. Unpublished doctoral dissertation, University of Auckland, Auckland, NZ.

Clay, M. M. (1967). The reading behavior of five-year-old children: A research report. New Zealand Journal of Educational Studies, 2, 11–31.

Clay, M. M. (1975). What did I write? Auckland, New Zealand: Heinemann.

Clay, M. M. (1991). Becoming literate: The construction of inner control. Portsmouth, NH: Heinemann.

Cochran-Smith, M. (1984). The making of a reader. Norwood, NJ: Ablex.

DeFord, D. (1994). Early writing: Teachers and children in reading recovery. Literacy, Teaching and Learning. Vol. 1, No. 1, p. 32.

Dewey, J. (1916). Democracy and education. New York: The Free Press.

Dyson, A. H. (1983). The role of oral language in early writing processes. Research in the Teaching of English, 17, 1–30.

Dyson, A. H. (1989). Multiple worlds of child writers: Friends learning to write. New York: Teachers College Press.

Dyson, A. H. (1990). The word and the world: Reconceptualizing written language development or do rainbows mean a lot to little girls? (Tech. Rep. No. 42). Berkeley, CA: University of California, Center for the Study of Writing.

Dyson, A. H., & Freedman, S. W. (1991). Writing. In J. Flood, J. M. Jensen, D. Lapp, & Jr. Squire (Eds.). Handbook of research on teaching the English language arts (pp. 754–774). New York: Macmillan.

Dyson, A. H. (1993). Social worlds of children learning to write in an urban primary school. New York: Teachers College Press.

Goodman, K. S., & Goodman, Y. (1979). Learning to read is natural. In L. B. Resnick & P. B. Weaver (Eds.). <u>Theory and practice of early reading</u>. Vol. 1 (pp. 137–154) Hillsdale, NJ: Lawrence Erlbaum.

Graves, D. H. (1983). <u>Writing: Teachers and children at work.</u> Portsmouth, NH: Heinemann.

Graves, D. H. (1990). <u>Discovering your own literacy.</u> Portsmouth, NH: Heinemann.

Green, J. L., & Harker, J. O. (1982). Reading to children: A communicative process. In J. A. Langer & M. T. Smith Burke (Eds.). <u>Reader meets author/ Bridging the gap: A psycholinguistic and sociolingustic perspective</u> (pp. 196–221). Newark, DE: International Reading Association.

Green, J., Dixon, C., Lin, L., Floriani, A., Bradley, M., Paxton, S., Mattern, C., and Bergamo, H. (1992). Constructing literacy in classrooms: Literate action as social accomplishment. In R. B. Ruddell, M. R. Ruddell, & H. Singer (Eds.). <u>Theoretical models and processes of reading</u> (4th ed., pp. 616–636). Newark, DE: International Reading Association.

Harste, J. C. (1994). Literacy as curricular converstations about knowledge, inquiry, and morality. In. R. B. Ruddell, M. R. Ruddell, & H. Singer (Eds.). <u>Theoretical models and processes of reading</u> (4th ed.) (pp. 1,220–1,242). Newark, DE: International Reading Association.

Harste, J. C., Burke, C. L., & Woodward, V. A. (1982). Children's language and world: Initial encounters with print. In J. A. Langer & In M. T. Smith-Burke (Eds.). <u>Reader meets author/Bridging the gap</u> (pp. 105–131). Newark, DE: International Reading Association.

Harste, J. C., Burke, C. L., & Woodward, V. A. (1984). <u>Language stories and literacy lessons.</u> Portsmouth, NH: Heinemann.

Harste, J. C., & Short, K. G. (1988). <u>Creating classrooms for authors.</u> Portsmouth, NH: Heinemann.

Heath, S. B. (1983). <u>Ways with words.</u> New York: Cambridge University Press.

Heller, C. (1990). <u>Women writers of the tenderloin</u> (Tech. Rep.) Berkeley, CA: University of California, Center for the Study of Writing.

Irwin, J. W., & Doyle, M. A. (1992). <u>Reading/writing connections: Learning from research.</u> Newark, DE: International Reading Association.

Jacobs, L. B. (1965). Telling stories to young children. In L. B. Jacobs (Ed.). <u>Using literature with young children</u> (pp. 15–20). New York: Teacher's College Press.

Johnson, D., & Johnson, R. (1975). <u>Learning together and alone.</u> Englewood Cliffs, NJ: Prentice Hall.

Johnson, D., & Johnson, R. (1985). The internal dynamics of cooperative learning groups. In R. Slavin, S. Sharon, S. Kagan, R. Hertz-Lazarowitz, C. Webb, & R. Schmuck (Eds.). <u>Learning to cooperate, cooperating to learn</u> (pp. 103–124). New York: Penium Press.

Martinez, M., & Teale, W. H. (1987). The ins and outs of a kindergarten writing program. <u>Reading Teacher,</u> 40, 444–451.

McLane, J., & McNamee, J. (1990). <u>Early literacy.</u> Cambridge, MA: Harvard University Press.

Moll, L. C. (1994). Literacy research in community and classrooms: A sociocultural approach. In R. B. Ruddell, & M. R. Ruddell (Eds.). <u>Theoretical models and proccesses of reading</u> (4th ed) (pp. 179–207). Newark, DE: International Reading Association.

Morrow, L. M. (1993). <u>Literacy development in the early years.</u> Boston: Allyn & Bacon.

Murray, D. (1989). Expecting the unexpected: Teaching myself—and others—to read and write. Portsmouth, NH: Bynton/Cook-Heinemann.

National Education Goals Panel. (1995). The national education goals report (ISBN 0-16-048364-6). Washington, DC: United States Government Printing Office.

Ninio, A., & Bruner, J. (1978). The achievement and antecedents of labelling. Journal of Child Language, 5, 1–15.

Riordan-Karlsson, M. E. (1996). Professional's guide: Motivating at-risk students. Teacher Created Materials, Westminister, CA.

Riordan-Karlsson, M. E. (1997). Negotiations, friendships, and chapter books: The influence of meaning authority, peer interaction, and student perceptions on reader motivation and meaning construction in a third grade classroom. Unpublished doctoral dissertation. University of California at Berkeley. Berkeley, CA.

Rogoff, B. (1990). Apprenticeship in thinking. New York. Oxford University Press.

Rosenblatt, L. M. (1978). The reader, the text, the poem: The transactional theory of the literary work. Carbondale, IL: Southern Illinois Press.

Ruddell, M. R., & Ruddell, R. B. (1994). Language acquisition and literacy processes. In R. B. Ruddell, M. R. Ruddell, & H. Singer (Eds.). Theoretical models and processes of reading (4th ed., pp. 616–636). Newark, DE: International Reading Association.

Ruddell, R. B., & Unrau, N. (1994). Reading as a meaning construction process: The reader, the text, and the teacher. In R.B. Ruddell, M. R. Ruddell, & H. Singer (Eds.). Theoretical models and processes of reading (4th ed., pp. 616–636). Newark, DE: International Reading Association.

Ruddell, R. B., & Ruddell, M. R. (1995). Teaching children to read and write. Boston, MA: Allyn and Bacon.

Seuss, Dr. (1957). The cat in the hat. New York: Random House.

Stotsky, S. (1983). Research on reading/writing relationships: A synthesis and suggested directions. Language Arts, 60, 627–643.

Sulzby, E. (1989). Assessment of writing and of children's language while writing. In L. Morrow & J. Smith (Eds.). The role of assessment and measurement in early literacy instruction (pp. 83–109). Englewood Cliffs. NJ: Prentice-Hall.

Sulzby, E. (1986). Writing and reading: Signs of oral and written language organization in the young child. In W. H. Teale & E. Sulzby (Eds). Emergent literacy: Writing and reading (pp. 50–89). Norwood, NH: Ablex.

Sulzby, E., & Teale, W. H. (1985). Writing development in early childhood. Educational Horizons, 64, 8–12.

Sulzby, E., Teale, W. H., & Kamberelis, G. (1989). Emergent writing in the classroom; Home and school connections. In D. S. Strickland & L. M. Morrow (Eds.). Emerging literacy: Young children learn to read and write (pp. 63–79). Newark, DE: International Reading Association.

Teale, W. H., & Sulzby E. (Eds.., (1986). Emergent literacy: Writing and reading. Norwood, NJ: Ablex.

Teale, W. H., & Sulzby, E. (1987). Literacy acquisition in early childhood: The roles of access and mediation in storybook reading. In D.A. Wagner (Ed.). The future of literacy in a changing world. (pp. 11–130). New York: Pergamon Press.

Temple, C., & Gillet, J. W. (1989). Language arts: Learning processes and teaching practices (2nd ed.) Glenview, IL: Scott, Foresman and Company.

Temple, C., Nathan, R., Temple, F., & Burris, N. A. (1993). The beginnings of writing (3rd ed.) Boston: Allyn & Bacon.

Turner, J., & Paris, S. (1995). How literacy tasks influence children's motivation for literacy. The Reading Teacher, 48, 662–673.

Vygotsky, L. (1978). Mind in society. Cambridge, MA: Harvard University Press.

Vygotsky, L. (1986). Thought and language (A. Kozulin, Trans. & Ed.) Cambridge, MA: MIT Press.

Wertsch, J. V. (1985). Vygotsky and the social formation of mind. Cambridge, MA: Harvard University Press.

Wertsch, J. V. (1991). Voices of the mind: A sociocultural approach to mediated action. Cambridge, MA: Harvard University Press.

Williams, J. M. (1995). Phonemic awareness. In Harris, T. L., & Hodges, R. E. (Eds.). The literacy dictionary (p. 185). Newark, DE: International Reading Association.

Wood, D., Bruner, J.S., & Ross, B. (1976). The role of tutoring in problem-solving. Journal of Child Psychology and Psychiatry, 17, 89–100.

Teacher Created Materials Reference List

TCM 2009 Writing Workshop Lessons and Activities for the Writing Process: Grades K–3

TCM 147 Activities for any Literature Unit—Primary

TCM 500 Write all About It—Grades 1–2–3

TCM 2316 Phonics, Phonemic Awareness, Word Recognition Activities

TCM 505 Jump into Journals